SEARCHING FOR SAM

A Father's Quest for Meaning

Timothy S. Johnson

Visit
www.searchingforsam.com
For A Special Message From The Author

105 150 Crowfoot Cres NW #1018 Calgary, AB T3G 3T2
Tel 1-888-824-7346   Fax (403) 241-6685

We are not human beings having
a spiritual experience.
We are spiritual beings having
a human experience.

Pierre Teilhard de Chardin
(1881-1955)

For Dawn

The most courageous person I know

CONTENTS

PROLOGUE

DANCING IN THE LIGHT

My two middle daughters, Laura and Alana, are sixteen months apart (Laura is older). One night an awesome thunder storm came rumbling, banging and crashing into my slumber. When I awoke, I thought immediately of Laura, then five years old. Our other children were very sound sleepers, but Laura was bothered even by subtle noises in the night and was downright frightened by thunder.

Pulling on my bath robe, I hurried down the hall to Laura's bedroom and found her quaking, in the fetal position, head underneath her blankets, eyes closed tight — scared to utter as much as a peep. As I gathered her into my arms, I spoke gentle, reassuring words. She clung to my neck like a burr to terrycloth.

Once back in my bed, I woke my wife, Dawn, and the two of us cuddled and loved Laura out of her fright. Suddenly, Laura said, "Alana's scared too!" This struck me as odd. Laura and Alana slept in seperate rooms... how could Laura know?

At that, I got up and went to see Alana, Laura's younger sister. I found her in the same condition as Laura had been in only moments before. I scooped up the clinging, trembling mute, but this time before going back to my room, I stopped to check on Juli and Sam who were both in deep, comfortable

9

dreamland. Back in our bed, Dawn on one side, me on the other, and the two pint-sized, trembling, milk-shake machines between us, we continued to ease them out of their waking nightmare.

I asked Laura: "How did you know Alana was scared? Did you hear her call out?"

"No," Laura said. "I just knew."

I found myself wondering: "How did she know?" After very little debate, the simple answer was, "She just knew."

She had a knowing, a feeling, a sense, an intuition, she was connected, she was aware.... She just "knew." Was this a "sixth sense" at work? A sense beyond sight, touch, smell, taste and hearing? Well let's say . . . maybe. Are such intuitions connected with premonitions? With mind-reading? With the moving of objects with the mind? What about communicating with passed-over spirits? And past-life regressions?

Unfortunately, I don't have the answers to these questions. My feeling is that we may well be multi-dimensional creatures possessed of all kinds of untapped abilities — but that, almost certainly, there is at least one more sense. This sense is not a gift given to the chosen few, but is one that can either expand and develop or atrophy to non-existence.

The intuition and knowingness I have witnessed in all my children as preschoolers, I have seen wane as they entered the rigid, left-brain-oriented school system: sit up straight, everyone line up, put up your hand to talk, two plus two is four, the square root of eighty-one is always nine, everyone on page thirty-seven, no exceptions.

As a parent, I feel it's important that I allow my children candid conversations, coloring outside the lines and as many right-brained, "creative" activities as I can. Music, art, drama . . . not to the exclusion of reading, 'riting and 'rithmetic, but to the acceptance and inclusion of creative, "other-sensory" activities. I want them not only to hang onto the sensory gifts they have, but to expand and develop them.

For me, as an adult, the task is harder. The secret, I feel, is not to imagine acquiring any new sense or senses, but rather to remember how to use the senses I was given. To remember how to quiet the voices in my head, to turn inward and listen . . . to go deeper.

Intuition has always played a role in my life, of course, as it does in everybody's. But I didn't become aware of its tremendous importance until six or seven years ago, when in my early thirties I hit a rough patch and did some intense personal work. That's when I began to conceive my intuition as a sort of fiber-optic cable carrying all the wonders and secrets of the universe. I see this intuitive cable as suspended and running through my life at a constant level. Being a visual person, I would draw it as a heavy pink line across this page at the middle.

My conscious mind, by contrast, I visualize as a jagged black line starting at the bottom of the page in the left hand corner, travelling almost straight upwards to the top of the page while moving slightly to the right. Once this black line hits the top, it immediately begins a rapid descent towards the bottom of the page, again moving only slightly to the right. It repeats this up-and-down action all the way across the page. This black line represents my conscious mind swinging from the highest of emotional highs to the lowest of heartbreaking lows, when I found myself disconnnected and withdrawn, alone in an intellectual wasteland.

Those points at which the jagged black line intersects with the heavy pink line indicate the times in my life when my head and heart line up. However briefly, I am calm, centred, grounded. During those times, the simplest yet most profound messages come to me, provided by my intuition — my "sixth sense," if you will. Not all of those messages are welcome. Yet even the darkest, most difficult insights, including those that arrive as part of a recurring premonition I've experienced over the years, arrive only when I am centred, grounded and connected with my intuition.

It is as if my fiber-optic intuition carries the purest white light of the universe. Through it runs every piece of information that I need or ever will need to evolve in this lifetime. Perhaps that is why the briefest of connections delivers such a thundering jolt of power and insight. For me, the challenge is to embrace my intuition — to find the courage and tenacity to hold a prism in front of the rushing white light and observe the rainbow of possibilities that explode before me.

The story I want to share with you is about facing the most daunting challenge that most human beings — certainly those who are loving parents — can imagine. It's a story about the sudden, untimely passing of my six-year-old son, Samuel Jess Johnson. It's about how I came to embrace, trust and follow my intuition, my sixth sense, and let it guide me through the valley of death. It's about how I learned to spend more time dancing in the light.

CHAPTER ONE

OMENS OF TRAGEDY

On the evening of April 7, 1999, in the heart of the Canadian Rockies, my wife and I parked our car in front of the massive Banff Springs Hotel and entered the lobby. The bellman was away, probably parking another guest's vehicle, so we dropped our car keys in the lock box as a sign instructed and began wending our way towards our room. The hotel was built in 1888 and even the most recent renovations featured almost-flawless recreations of Victorian design, art and decor. We strolled along hand in hand, stopping every few yards to admire a fresco, enjoy a painting or gaze out a window at the surrounding mountains. A casual observer might have taken us for honeymooners who didn't have a care in the world.

In truth, I was finding it difficult to relax. All day long, something had been bothering me. Dawn and I had rolled out of bed around five thirty — even before the youngest of our five children. We'd showered and eaten a light breakfast. By the time the caregiver arrived at six, we were ready to make the ninety-minute drive to Banff, the mountain resort in which I'd arranged to attend a one-day workshop. After that, we planned to enjoy an extended two day vacation at the Springs, taking advantage of room service, the movie channel and an alluring Spa Package.

As I turned to walk out the door, Dawn remembered that we'd promised to wake our six-year-old to say goodbye: "We have to wake Sam."

Even as she spoke, Sam stumbled sleepily out of the kids' bedroom, rubbing his eyes. He said, "You guys were going to wake me, right? So I could say goodbye?"

Dawn said, "Of course we were."

He gave Dawn a huge hug and a nice kiss on the cheek and said, "I love you. You're the best Mom I ever had." Then he came over to me and did the same. I gave him a gentle swat on the behind and chased him back into the bedroom. I tucked him neatly into bed and said, "I sure love you, little man!"

"I love you too, Dad," he replied.

Dawn and I finished packing our belongings and piled them into our car.

We said goodbye to the caregiver, Barbara, giving her our itinerary and phone numbers where we could be reached. The last thing Dawn said to her was: "The kids are not to go anywhere on the property unattended. Someone must be with them at all times."

Two winters before, when we had moved to Millarville, several neighbours had complained about wild cougars entering their yards and carrying away small dogs and even sheep for consumption. This news had triggered an awareness program that all residents had taken and then followed to the letter. The previous spring, Dawn and I had discovered a female bear, up and about in a nasty mood after a long hibernation, on our porch licking the inside of tomato cans but clearly looking for something much more filling.

As a result, talking to the caregiver, Dawn drove home her point: "The kids are not even to go alone to the Quonset hut (one hundred feet away)."

Barbara said she understood.

Meanwhile, something was bothering me. I

didn't know what it was, but I walked out onto the deck and drained the hot tub. Levi, our 18-month-old, was a master at getting into things and I had a sense our home would be safer with the tub empty.

We drove the half kilometer down the steep hill to the bottom of our property, where I'd recently built a blue teepee to act as a shelter for the kids while waiting for the schoolbus. But still something was bothering me. Something really eating at me . . . needling me. I stopped at the Texas gate, put the car in park and said, "Dawn, something is really bugging me. Something doesn't feel right."

She said, "What?"

"I don't think we should go. I feel very uncomfortable."

"What do you feel uncomfortable about?"

"I don't know what it is."

"Well, you know we haven't been away together for a long time. You've been working so hard. Probably you're just over-tired."

I shifted from my heart, and my feeling that something was wrong, to my head, which told me I was imaginging things, and said, "Yeah, you're right." I shook off what was troubling me. "I've got a full-day conference to attend and we certainly do need the time away together. I'm sure everything will be okay."

I slapped the car into gear, swung onto the highway and headed west.

From the community in which we live, Millarville, Alberta, you can see the Canadian Rockies looming massive and white-capped on the horizon. We followed a two-lane highway to the trans-Canada, and then followed that for an hour, driving through the National Park gates, and then on into the town of Banff, and ultimately to the historical Canadian Pacific hotel where the conference was being held.

We met our friends, Jim and Janice Armitage, at

the front door of the hotel. Jim and I were going to spend the day with Dan Sullivan, a business strategic coach with whom I'd been working for eight years. Janice and Dawn would spend the day cross-country skiing. This was early April, after all, nearing the end of the season, and the sun was blazing down in a bright blue sky.

After checking in and dropping our bags in our rooms, we went our separate ways. My sense of unease didn't go away, but kept eating at me. Something felt wrong though I didn't know what — but instead of exploring this intuition, I listened to my intellect and speculated that maybe I was coming down with a cold. Together with two dozen other entrepreneurs all seeing how they could improve on themselves and their businesses, I worked through the eight-hour Strategic Coach program, applying myself to personal-development exercises and strategies.

As four-thirty approached, I felt a strange rush, an influx of nervous energy. Usually when this happens, it's because I've drunk too much coffee. But today, around 9 a.m., I'd decided to drink only water and had done just that for the rest of the day.

When the event finally ended, Jim and I got talking about a competitor of mine. Suddenly, I found myself tearing strips off this guy in a way that was completely out of character for me. I was really pumped and unleashed quite a scathing critique. As soon as Jim and I parted, I felt bad about what I'd said. I didn't feel right in my stomach.

Back in our room, I found Dawn relaxing on the king-sized bed, propped up with pillows and watching music videos — something she thoroughly enjoys when we are away from the kids. In about an hour, we were slated to meet the Armitages for dinner. But I found I couldn't sit still. I felt so energized that I fell to the floor and did twenty-five quick pushups.

Dawn said, "Tim, what's got into you?"

"I don't know. All this pent-up energy. I don't know what to do with it. Want to go for a walk?"

" I've been skiing all day, remember? But you go ahead. I'll meet you at the restaurant."

Briskly, I walked the half mile into town and then strode along the Bow River, trying in vain to enjoy the outdoors while killing just over an hour. Arriving at the restaurant, I found I was still highly energized. I decided to have a beer to see if that would settle me down, relax me a bit. The beer had no effect so I ordered a scotch. As I started to drink it, Jim Armitage arrived with his wife, Janice. Right away, I apologized for having vented about my competitor. Jim told me not to worry about it, but I said, "No, no, I don't know what got into me — sorry about that."

Dawn arrived almost immediately and we all four agreed to have supper in the lounge, where a National Hockey League game was playing on TV: Edmonton Oilers versus the Calgary Flames, one of those classic rivalries that turn up in professional sports. The game didn't mean much to the Flames, who now figured out of the playoff picture, but for the Oilers, it meant plenty. From where I sat, I could chat with the others while keeping one eye on the game — a perfect arrangement considering that my mind was still in turmoil. I didn't know why, but I felt incapable of carrying on a meaningful conversation.

Shortly after we sat down, Dawn reminded me that we were supposed to phone the children at the Quonset hut — a separate building at home in which I had my office and where the kids usually came to play video games or use the VCR. Shortly after seven o'clock we phoned but got no answer. That seemed odd: the kids should have finished their supper and have started their movie. At seven-thirty we phoned again — both the Quonset hut and our home. No answer. Eight o'clock we phoned: no answer. Eight-thirty: no answer. Nine o'clock: still no answer.

A terrible feeling of unease washed over me, the same sense of dread I'd felt that morning at the Texas gate, when I'd wanted not to depart. Again I shrugged it off, choosing intellect over intuition — though with less conviction. Worriedly, we all four agreed: probably the telephone had come unplugged. Or maybe the ringer had been accidentally switched off. Anyway, no need to worry. Finally, the hockey game wound up. We settled the bill and the Armitages suggested we go to a different spot where we could hear a band, maybe enjoy a nightcap.

Dawn and I didn't feel in the mood. We took a rain check and drove back to the Banff Springs. Having dropped our car keys in the night check-in box, as a sign instructed, we arrived at our room and found it pitch dark except for the crimson pulse of a telephone light indicating that a message was waiting. I no sooner saw that pulsing light than I felt a charge shoot through me. Instantly, I intuited that the waiting message was linked to the uneasy feeling that had been gnawing at me all day with such dogged persistence. My intellect responded: Not to worry. It is just the hotel wondering if the room is okay.

I didn't want to admit it to myself, or to alarm Dawn, but at some level I felt afraid to take the message. To Dawn, as I stepped into the bathroom, I said casually, "Why don't you phone and see what that the message is?"

In the bathroom, I started to brush my teeth but found myself being quiet as a mouse to eavesdrop. I could not make out what Dawn was saying, but her tone and inflection made the hairs stand up on the back of my neck. I stepped out of the bathroom as she put down the phone: "Tim, the RCMP are on their way up to see us."

CHAPTER TWO

PRAYING FOR A MIRACLE

I believe that the human mind processes information infinitely faster than the most powerful computer on our planet. As the last word left Dawn's mouth, I formulated and discounted multiple scenarios as to why the RCMP wanted to talk to us. Were they summoning me about unpaid parking tickets? Or maybe a long-forgotten speeding ticket? Those didn't fit so I discounted them. I had already dismissed the idea that they were informing me, the next of kin, about the passing of my mother or my step-father.

I had discounted thoughts about my siblings, that perhaps one of them had been fatally injured in an accident and needed to be identified. I continued reasoning while the obvious ate away at me. (It was as if one part of my mind knew exactly what message awaited me and that part was patiently waiting for the other part to finish its flimsy check list). This was something serious, extremely serious. Somehow, I knew it involved my children. When I checked my gut on the events over the past few days, my brain drew a single, icy, stark conclusion. Suddenly, I knew: I was about to receive grave news about my son Sam.

My knees buckled as if someone had hit me in the bottom of the stomach with a baseball bat. I fell onto the bed feeling sick inside, queasy, as if a main artery had been slashed and my blood and energy were pouring out of me. I knew what I was about to hear, but already my intellect was scoffing, demanding proof. I grabbed the telephone.

"Tim, what are you doing? The police are on their way!"

"I can't wait! I need to know what's going on right now!"

The hospital nearest our residence in Millarville is at Black Diamond, a slightly larger town. After securing and dialing the number, I told the woman who answered: "This is Tim Johnson! I need to speak to the doctor in charge, the doctor on call."

"One moment." There was a quickness, an urgency in the way she acknowledged me — an inflection suggesting she knew who I was and why I was calling. My intuition was bang on!

A man's voice said, "This is Doctor Jones."

Again I identified myself, adding: "I understand you have one of my children there! I need to know what's going on."

The doctor went to protocol: "Have you talked to the RCMP?"

Another electric charge went through me: "No. The RCMP are on their way but they're taking an unbelievable amount of time. They're not here yet."

"You need to talk to the RCMP."

"Listen! I don't have time for this bullshit routine! I need to know what's wrong with one of my children."

The doctor remained very calm and collected: "I can't tell you anything until the RCMP have spoken to you."

"For God's sake, man!" Without missing a beat, I followed my instincts: "I need to know what's going on with my son Sam!"

"Then you know," he said.

"Well, I've heard — but not through the RCMP."

The doctor abandoned protocol and dropped the

bomb: "Your son Samuel ventured out onto your ice-covered pond in Millarville. He fell through the ice and spent about forty-five minutes in the water." He spoke as if there were no breaks, no periods at the end of any of his sentences. "He has been airlifted to the Foothills General Hospital in Calgary and they are working on him right now."

I dropped the receiver and fell to my knees beside the bed: "Please, God, no! Please, God, not Sam."

I sensed an enormous whirling pool, a terrible maelstrom of emotion, surging below me and to my left. It was vast, dark and furious. It was calling, inviting me to plunge, to let myself go and rage around the room breaking lamps and screaming obscenities. Just as I started my destructive dive, Dawn's voice pulled me back into the room: "Tim, what's going on? What's happening?"

Dawn was frantic. I couldn't look at her. If I could have, I would have seen terror on her face. I struggled to give her the sketchy details while looking away, knowing that if I met her eyes, I might completely break down. Finally, with a mighty effort, I pulled myself together: "Get your bags packed!" I cried. "We're going to see Sam!"

"But we have to wait for the RCMP."

"Dawn, we're not waiting for anybody."

We scooped up our bags and ran to the entranceway. The key for our car was still in the lock box. We were stymied. I picked up the phone to the front desk and said, "You need to get somebody here in thirty seconds or less to open this lock box! We have an emergency and have to leave right now."

As I hung up the telephone, I considered kicking in the side of the lock box so we could leave immediately. As I stepped back and cocked my leg, I realized that I had better keep my composure. The last thing I wanted, one hour and fifteen minutes away from the Foothills General Hospital, was to be detained by the RCMP (who were going to be arriving any minute) for destroying property belonging to the Banff Springs Hotel.

Within a few moments, which seemed an eternity, a hotel security guard arrived jostling his keys. As he opened the lock box, two RCMP constables turned the corner, one male and one female. It made sense to me that if you were going to inform a couple that a loved one was in critical condition, or had just passed away, you had better have a man to talk to the husband and a woman to talk to the wife. As they approached they asked, "Are you folks Tim and Dawn Johnson?"

The male said they had some news regarding someone in our family. I quickly responded that I understood my son had fallen through the ice on the family pond and that he had been airlifted to Calgary. The female RCMP officer added some new information: "Your son was discovered as soon as he fell in the water. When they took him out of the pond, his body temperature was low but his heart was beating."

Amid the chaos of the last few moments, and high above the emotional maelstrom, I felt a life-line of hope run through my mind. Mentally, I reached up and grabbed hold. Stunned, I repeated: "His heart is beating, he's cold, he's been airlifted out . . . so he's okay."

The constable said, "That's all I know, that's all I have for you."

We hustled out to the parking lot, unlocked the vehicle, and rifled our bags into the back seat. The male constable came to me and said, "Would you like us to drive for you? Would you like us to give you an escort?" At the back of my mind, I thought, I'm going to drive about fifteen kilometers above the speed limit all the way into town. I don't want a constable driving my vehicle at any lesser speed while I'm doing a slow burn in the back seat. I gathered every ounce of composure left to me, knowing that if I didn't come off calm, cool and collected, this request would turn into a command. I turned to him and politely said, "No, that's fine, we'll be okay."

We left the parking lot at just slightly under the posted speed. Once on the highway, I decided to set the cruise control so I wouldn't get ahead of myself and start to speed at a rate that would get us stopped by a different RCMP officer — perhaps somebody who didn't know where we were going or why.

Immediately, Dawn started making calls on the cellphone. First she phoned the RCMP in Turner Valley, another town near Millarville, and talked with the sergeant in charge. I could hear only her questions and not his responses, which drove me crazy, my mind formulating numerous options. After she hung up, she summarized what the sergeant had told her. Sam was found in the water and unconscious. He was found right away. The rescue workers recovered him within one minute after arriving on the scene. His heart was beating. His core temperature was very low. He was airlifted to the Foothills Hospital. They were working very hard to save his life.

Everyone was saying the same thing. Details were sketchy but I clung to the lifeline of hope — there was hope! Dawn kept working the telephone. She called various neighbours and checked on our other four children and the doctor who was working on Sam. Each time she hung up the telephone, she brought me up to speed. I held my left hand to my mouth as I drove, biting my knuckles. I knew if I removed it, I would start screaming: WHAT'S GOING ON HERE? WHO THE HELL IS IN CHARGE? I said nothing. I concentrated on getting to the hospital safely and as quickly as possible.

Finally, we pulled into the parking lot. We jumped

out of the car and ran to the emergency entrance. At the door, by total coincidence, we encountered a security guard from Millarville — a man named Joe Perot whose son Dylan ironically was in Sam's kindergarten class. He looked at us with a blank, stricken face and said: "Come this way, please. The doctor wants to bring you up to speed on Sam."

I searched his manner, his voice, his inflection... there was hope!

We followed Joe into the waiting room. "Listen, I can't tell you much," he said. "Only that Sam is alive and the doctors are working on him. Please wait here. The doctors want to see you."

Appearing again, immediately below and to the left, was the mouth of that terrible maesltrom. There seemed to be no end to the grief it offered. My mind prompted me to jump to the worst possible conclusion. It wanted me to plunge. I set my feet, took a deep breath and wrestled my mind to a standstill.

The waiting lasted an eternity. What was happening? Please, somebody tell us! Finally, the doctors in charge of Sam, "Doctor Smith" and "Doctor Abel," came into the waiting room and sat down across from Dawn and me. They wore green scrub clothes not unlike those you see doctors wearing on TV. Dr. Smith had tucked his hair into a green cap that matched his top and pants and he also wore a mask; the bottom half done up around his neck, the other half hanging down over his chest.

The doctor Dawn had talked to by cell phone, Dr. Smith, assumed the role of spokesperson. He looked to be in his late thirties. Focused and articulate, he laid it on the line for us. "Your son Samuel was rescued from under fifteen feet of water by a Calgary diver. Sam had no pulse. He was loaded onto a waiting STARS air ambulance and airlifted to us here at the hospital. Before he was placed on board the helicopter, his heart started again by itself. His body temperature was 17 degrees Celsius (63 Fahrenheit), compared with a normal temperature of 37 (98.6 Fahrenheit). Once Sam reached the hospital, we immediately hooked him up to our bypass machine to introduce oxygen into his system and warm up his blood."

At that, my mind raced. A few months before, my mother had undergone heart bypass surgery. I knew that in order to hook a person up to a bypass machine, doctors must make an incision from the top of the breast bone to the bottom of the breast bone, open the chest cavity and then connect the bypass machine to the heart. I knew a bit about what he was talking about, and although he had just said, "hooked him up to a bypass machine," I understood that this was an intensely serious, major surgical procedure. The doctors were literally fighting for my son's life! I also knew that if Sam had been under water for any period of time, had been airlifted to the hospital and had only now been connected to a bypass machine, then most likely he would suffer critical damage to his vital organs. Doctor Smith said, "What we're doing now is introducing oxygen into his blood and warming him up slowly at the same time. Once he reaches normal body temperature, we can assess if there is any damage to other areas of his body. We'll bring him to that level, assess him, then take him off the bypass machine. At that point, he'll have to make a go of it on his own. That's the critical point . . . he is a very sick boy."

At that moment, part of me wanted to cry out: "Take me to him! I want to be with my boy! I want to hold his hand, I want to be part of this!" At the same time, I realized that my son was in the care of the finest professionals in Calgary. The last thing they needed was one or both of us coming apart at the seams in the operating room while they were doing their best to save Sam's life. Suddenly, I faced the most daunting decision of my life: Do I demand to be taken to my son? Or do I stay in the waiting room and let the doctors do their work? I thanked Doctor Smith, told him that our thoughts and prayers were with him, and let him return to our son.

As the door clicked shut behind him, I looked across the room at Dawn. Like me, she had aged twenty years in the past two hours. Looking at her, I silently asked God to intervene. I asked God to lift our burden, to take all the magic he had planned for me for the rest of my life, to round it all up and bring it into that operating room and breathe life, breathe magic, breathe all that is good back into my boy.

I wanted a miracle, but I thought of it as magic. I thought of the magic that has been sprinkled through my almost forty years — the magic that not only brought five wonderful children to and through me, but that also brought Dawn and I together. I thought of the magic of our first chance meeting, the magic of the day when I met my soul mate, my best friend, the love of my life....

CHAPTER THREE

THE MAGIC OF LOVE

My first "real" job out of university was working at a newly constructed, high tech, canola-oil refinery in the thriving metropolis of Wainwright, Alberta (population: 5,000). I worked as a process co-ordinator, donning less-than-sexy blue cotton shirt, pants and hard hat to run one of four stream-driven processes involved in refining vegetable oil.

Although I enjoyed this salaried position, I always saw it as temporary — a front for a credit rating, if you will. I was ambitious, bent on doing well financially and spending as little of my life as possible punching a time clock and making somebody else rich. The twelve-hour shifts at the plant enabled me to take home $2,000 a month while giving me large blocks of spare time.

In that spare time I began to purchase real estate "fixer-uppers." I would buy the rental property with little or no money down, then clean, renovate and paint before renting it out for more than the mortgage payment. I'd refinance the property with the built-up equity from renovating, find another property and repeat the process. I developed an eye for diamonds in the rough and within four years I'd accumulated a portfolio of thirteen sound rental properties generating $3,000 per month positive cash flow and a net worth exceeding $250,000.

In Wainwright (two hours east of the Alberta capital of Edmonton), the third Saturday in June has traditionally been reserved for an annual Rodeo & Stampede Dance. By 1987, I'd been living in town for four years and hadn't attended any of these dances. But that summer, having recently bought a cowboy hat and a new pick-up truck, I felt compelled to mosey on over for a spell.

After a few cold ones and some laughs with buddies from the plant, I felt ready to go home and catch a few winks before my Sunday day-shift. As I walked towards the door, I noticed a small crowd of people having a good time. One young woman in particular caught my eye — a tall, leggy brunette with whom I found myself on the dance floor a moment later. As we two-stepped around the hockey rink (converted by sawdust into a dance floor) laughing and exchanging names, I realized that I was totally at ease with this Dawn.

The band finished and, as was customary, couples started walking arm-in-arm around the dance floor waiting for the next number. I held out my arm and as Dawn put hers in mine I knew in that instant I had met the woman of my dreams — my confidante, my friend, my soul mate, my wife! Magic snapped and crackled around us. That moment remains vivid for me. I can still recall what Dawn was wearing (a white button-down cotton shirt and black blue jeans), what she said...everything! Dawn taught elementary school and was about to begin her well-earned summer vacation....

That entire summer, I would work my shifts at the plant, look after my properties and rather than sleep, spend time with Dawn. We played, romped, and frolicked the summer away like a couple of river otters. For the first time in my life I was head-over-heels in love. I had boundless energy and everywhere I went people would say, "What's got into you boy... are you in love?"

"Yep," I would say. "With that good-looking Dawn Szoke girl."

I reveled in the love, the energy . . . the magic of it all.

Dawn was raised on a ranch just outside of the small town of Hardisty, Alberta, along with five siblings. She is the type of girl who can put on a pair of blue jeans, roll up her sleeves and work side by side with me all day on a renovation, then put on pearls, pumps and a cocktail dress and simply take my breath away. She has a natural ease with herself and because of that other people, including those who have just met her, feel warm and comfortable in her presence. After an evening out, we would often talk about our dreams, hopes and plans until sun-up, discovering, for example, that we both wanted a large family.

That autumn, I made reservations for Dawn and me at Calgary's Inn on Lake Bonavista, the finest, most romantic restaurant I knew. I insisted on a corner table with an enchanting view of the lake and set the stage by holding Dawn's hand, telling her over the candle-lit table how wonderful she was and how special the moments we spent together. When I got to the line I'd been practicing for weeks, I could barely squeak it out: "Would you . . . would you like to spend the rest of your life with me?"

I thought, oh God, I hope she got the gist of that because I don't think I can repeat it. I was dying a thousand deaths. I really had no idea what she was going to say. Finally, after what seemed forever, Dawn said, "I'd love to!" The candle light danced in her eyes and, as she opened the blue velvet box I produced, her lovely face was charged with wonder, excitement and anticipation: "Ooooh, Tim!" She slipped on her new engagement ring and admired its many facets as they sparkled and shone in the flickering light.

We held hands, basking in the ambiance of the moment. Then the strangest thing happened: we looked around and discovered we were alone — that there wasn't another patron in the place. Earlier, when we'd entered the restaurant, the place had been jam-packed full to overflowing. Now, the tables were all set for the next day, a cleaner was vacuuming the carpet and our waiter, drained after a full and busy night, was smiling and wishing us a good evening. Outside in the cool night air, we burst out laughing. For the last five hours, we had been completely lost in each other. For us, Time itself had stood still.

On February 6, 1988, Dawn and I were married.

The following spring, we packed up all our worldly possessions and moved two hours west to the city of Edmonton, leaving behind not only loved ones but my soft, cosy, salaried job. With me, I took my passion for buying and selling real estate. I became a licensed realtor and, almost overnight, gained a strong following of clients. In my first month as a realtor, I earned more in commissions than I had earned in my best twelve months as an engineer. With the welcome responsibility of a new wife and a baby on the way, I threw myself headlong into my career.

CHAPTER FOUR

SAYING GOODBYE TO SAM

The night of April 7, 1999 remains a jumble in my mind. News had spread fast and soon friends and family arrived and joined us in the waiting room at Foothills Hospital. On arrival, they all wanted to know how Sam was making out. Then they wanted to tell us how they had reacted to the news. For example, one well-meaning woman said: "We saw this on the news, and we just knew it was Sam, and we were horrified." Something in the back of my mind said: "You were horrified, you were horrified? We're the parents! Can't you suspend your self-preoccupation for an instant and maybe ask, 'What can we do? How can we help?'"

I realized that anger was creeping into my attitude. Outwardly, I remained cool and relayed what the doctor had told us: all we could do now was to wait, pray and see what happened. Joe Perot returned and showed us into a different waiting area — one reserved for immediate family. I bid everyone else a good night, thanked people for their support, prayers, and concerns, and told them we would inform everyone as soon as we found out more. Dawn and I entered the second waiting area with my sister, Gina, her husband, Brian, and my youngest sister, Judy.

A chaplain arrived and said he was there to pray

with us, to talk with us and just to be with us if we wished. He shared some positive statistics about people spending time in water: the younger they were, the better chance they had of recovering. He said numerous people were praying for Sam and our family during this difficult time. He was very upbeat and positive and once again I found myself beginning to hope: maybe Sam would pull through, after all.

As we waited for news of our son's condition, Dawn and I stood beside an aquarium and watched the fish swim back and forth. I noticed her reflection in the glass: she was deeply immersed in shock and disbelief. She reminded me of a conversation I'd had with my mother a few years earlier: "Tim, you promise me: if ever I'm put on a life-support system, you'll tell the doctors to unplug me...promise?"

Although I had made this promise, it weighed heavily. One day, almost in passing, I mentioned it to our lawyer over lunch. He said, "Well, Tim, heaven forbid that situation should ever develop...you wouldn't be able to do a thing. Your mother needs to complete what's called 'a living will' or a 'personal directive.'"

Once my mother had completed this document, I found comfort in knowing that, come what may, her wishes would be honored. Not long afterwards, Dawn and I also completed living wills, stating clearly how we wished the situation to be handled should we ever find ourselves in such a situation. Now, as I stood at the aquarium, I realized that the doctors might indeed come to us and say that our son was hanging on by a thread — that there was damage to his kidneys, his other organs, perhaps his brain, and he was on life-support and would be for the rest of his life. I knew that if this became a reality, the only thing my energetic, fun-loving, rambunctious, playful, bubbly, rough-and-tumble son would want, if he could make the choice on his own, would be to pass into the next realm without interference.

As I finished that thought, the telephone rang. A woman asked for Tim or Dawn Johnson. She said Dr. Smith would like to see us now and gave us directions. We should exit the waiting room, turn left, follow the yellow line until we reached a blue line, turn right there and follow the blue line to another waiting area. Intuitively, I was already aware of the news we were going to hear when we reached the end of the blue line. The age of innocence was about to end.

I told those in the waiting room that Dawn and I were going to talk with the doctor and would return when we had news. My wife looked at me as if to ask whether I had been given pertinent information on the telephone. Without her asking, I said, "No, I don't have any news . . . they just want to see us."

We wandered the corridors, going back and forth through different doors while following yellow, then green, then red lines. Maybe unconsciously I wished to avoid the inevitable, but in any case I couldn't find the correct area. Finally, a nurse led us into an empty waiting room. After a while, escorted by Joe, two women arrived — obviously psychological support staff, though they wore no uniforms and looked stricken. One look at them told me all my instincts had been bang on.

As if on cue, the two doctors we had met entered the room. One asked the other if he had anything he wished to say. The younger man said, "Yes." Visibly shaken, he proved unable to continue. The older man, Doctor Smith, probably in an effort to begin, recapitulated his previous statements. He told us again that when Sam had been recovered from the pond he had a core temperature of 17 degrees Celsius (63 Fahrenheit), where normally it should 37 (98.6 Fahrenheit). By the time he arrived at the hospital, his heart had restarted on its own but his lungs remained full of water from the pond.

The previous summer, when a friend and I had rented scuba gear and explored that pond, I had been stunned by two findings. First, even though we dove at mid-summer, during the hottest part of the year, the water remained amazingly frigid. Second, in the deepest part of the pond (nineteen feet down), partly because of the depth but mostly because of the sheer murkiness, when I held my hand in front of my face mask, I couldn't see it. I looked up and couldn't see sunlight. . . I couldn't see anything.

Now the doctor explained that, if a person is immersed in water while conscious, a mammalian diving reflex prevents water or floating debris from entering the lungs. Because Sam, after submitting to hypothermia, had slipped into unconsciousness, this reflex did not kick in. His lungs had filled with frigid, squalid water. As the doctor reviewed the efforts they'd made to try to save Sam, I found myself mentally screaming: "Please, doctor! Just get to the bottom line on this!"

And all too soon he did: "So, after warming his blood, after feeding oxygen through his blood, after working from the time we got him, around quarter to eight last night, to one thirty this morning, we took him off the bypass machine…he was simply unable to sustain life. I am very sorry to tell you that your son didn't make it."

The room was silent, utterly still. Nobody moved, nobody breathed.

Time ceased to exist. The silence lasted forever… agonizing, simply unbearable.

Dawn turned to me: "Tim."

That single syllable carried more emotion, more meaning, than any ten thousand words I have ever heard or ever expect to hear. Then, into my heart and out of my mouth came these words: "You know what? . . . He had a good life."

We stared into each other's eyes.

To the doctors, Dawn said, "Can we see him?"

"Yes, of course. They are getting him ready. They'll be just a few moments."

Did I go into shock? I don't know. Certainly, I felt numb. And I found it impossible to express any emotion. Dawn said: "What are we going to do?"

"We are going to go and be with our son one last time. Then, we are going to gather up our family and go home." To Dr. Smith, I said, "We'd really like to see Sam."

"Yes, of course," he said. "I'll see if they're ready."

The two doctors left. Politely, I told the two women that we wanted just to be alone, but maybe they could let us know when Sam was ready?

Dawn and I waited alone and in silence. I have no idea how long we waited but eventually Joe Perot knocked on the door. He led us to a small room and pulled back the drapes and there was Sam, our son. A pale green sheet had been pulled up and folded neatly just beneath his arms. His arms rested on top of the sheet. I knew that Sam's chest had been cut open and perhaps sewn back together, perhaps bound with gauze. But I felt no need to see this. Having entered, Dawn moved instinctively to his right side.

Two nurses and Joe Perot remained in the room. I said, "We'd just like our privacy now, if you don't mind." They protested, offered to remain and just be there for us, but I said no thanks: "We'd just like to be with Sam, by ourselves, please."

Alone with our son, we experienced a quiet, tender moment of unbelievable gravity. Somewhat to my surprise, Sam's face was Sam's face. It was his, but it didn't have that healthy pinkish glow to it — it was pale. When I took Sam's hand, it was his hand. I studied the details — the cuticles, the dirt beneath his fingernails, some words to a game that he and his sisters had written. I held his limp hand in mine as I had so many different times, either at night time or carrying him from the couch to the bed. His hand felt that way... yet slightly different. It was cool to the touch, like when he was a baby and I would go in the middle of the night to cover him after he had kicked off all his blankets. It was cool and subtly different. I could feel no life in it.

Dawn was speaking to Sam, gently brushing his hair. For a while it seemed like the kind of conversation Dawn and I had indulged in many times when he was sleeping. Except that the gravity of the room, of the situation, was so immense, so overwhelming. As we spoke to Sam, we started a practice that we still continue: we speak to him knowing that some part of him is absent, yet believing also that he is still there, still listening.

We spoke to Sam for a long time. At one point I noticed some bubbles coming out of his nose, milky white and tinged with pink — obviously the result of work the doctors had done. I took a nearby Kleenex and wiped them away. We carried on for a while and then Dawn switched gears and began struggling, really struggling. Not knowing what else to do, I asked her if maybe it was time for us to leave. She said, "Yes, maybe it is — but can we stay a little longer?"

"We can stay as long as you want," I said.

We remained with Sam until Dawn said, "Okay, I'm ready, Tim. I'm ready to go."

We both kissed our son, touched him and said goodbye . . . .

As we left, I couldn't feel my feet or my hands. I felt as if I'd been anaesthetized. I knew that I was walking but not that I was moving. In the hall, one of the hospital administrators stopped us and offered his condolences. He added: "I think it's only fair to let you know that this tragedy has attracted a lot of television and radio coverage. The media will be informed right away of the passing of your son."

Those words shook me out of my dream-like state and jolted me back into reality. Suddenly, I felt a terrible sense of responsibility — a responsibility for phoning six, eight, perhaps as many as twelve people to let them know about the passing of our son, breaking the news to loved ones before they heard it on the radio or saw it on television.

The administrator also said that if we were thinking of donating Sam's body, or parts of Sam's body, then we should give permission right away. If we waited, not much could be used. Dawn looked at me reassuringly and I told the administrator to please go ahead and use whatever could be used of Sam's body to help somebody else. We signed the forms and walked back down the blue line to the yellow line into the waiting room.

There, I had to do the most difficult thing I have ever done, something that required every ounce of courage I possessed. I had to look into the eyes of someone I love and tell them that someone they loved had just died. This was a task I would perform many times in the next twenty-four hours. Now, I looked at Judy, Gina and Brian and said, "Sam passed away about an hour and a half ago."

They said many things: how sorry they were, how devastated. Could they do anything to help? I said no: the hospital was caring for Sam now. I thanked them for coming and for being there for Sam. Dawn and I made our way out of the hospital and back to the car. The time had come to drive home to Millarville and gather together our remaining children....

CHAPTER FIVE

DISCOVERING MILLARVILLE

Dawn and I discovered Millarville in the spring of 1996. Clients had asked me to investigate the towns and villages south and west of Calgary, the site of the 1988 Winter Olympics and the city in which I was born and raised. I had expected most residents to be farmers and ranchers but found that, almost without exception, the new families moving into these out-lying areas comprised married couples between the ages of thirty-five and fifty with 2.2 kids, a minivan, a sport-utility vehicle, a dog, two cats and a pony. Baby Boomers tired of the Big City Rat Race had been pulling up stakes and moving to acreages outside of town. Often commuting, either by car or modem, into Calgary to work, they'd chosen to raise their children in a more traditional, family-oriented, rural-community setting.

While conducting this survey, I stopped for a soft drink in a hamlet called Millarville. It boasted a spectacular view of the Rocky Mountains and a population of seventy-three. Friendly, down-home, laid-back — it was love at first sight. One week later, Dawn and I returned together to look around.

The eight years we'd spent in Edmonton had been good ones — though we'd known some rocky times, too. In the fall of 1991, we had experienced an especially difficult period — one that precipitated a "mid-course correction." In our private life, we were expecting our third child. As a realtor, my business and income continued to grow, but now at considerable cost. It was dominating my time and my life. I was gaining some "ugly pounds" from eating poorly, at the wrong time of day, and not exercising enough, if at all. Dawn was complaining about me not being around as much and often the kids were fast asleep by the time I got home from work.

Growing up, I had internalized the notion of gaining self-worth by being a good provider. Now, a growing part of me was screaming for a better, more meaningful relationship with my wife and kids. The turning point came one Sunday. The whole family had been invited to share in a birthday celebration at a local park. We arrived around noon. The day was gorgeous, the sun was shining, not a cloud in the sky....

Then my pager went off. I returned the call and learned that an important client was in town for the day and wished to write a "quick-and-easy" offer on a house. He said, "It'll only take a moment." I told the sad, gloomy faces of my family that I wouldn't be gone long, jumped in a cab and waved goodbye. The quick-and-easy offer kept me going until 11 p.m. but I closed the deal. Arriving home, I somewhat stupidly expected Dawn to congratulate me, offer me a cold beer and ask how I'd done it.

Instead, I found a note that said: "Find somewhere else to sleep!"

I knew something had to change

The following week, I received an invitation to an introductory workshop with Dan Sullivan, the well-known "Strategic Coach." He promised to show self-employed "coachies" earning more than $100,000 per year how to achieve higher incomes while reducing stress and enjoying more free time. At the session itself, while talking about family, he produced the clincher when he addressed parents in the audience, saying: "Kids don't want quality time from Mom and Dad — they want quantity time."

When the student is ready, the teacher arrives. I remembered how between business meetings, I would give the kids fifteen minutes to play baseball in a nearby park. On Saturday mornings, before rushing off to work, I would make breakfast — sometimes before the last of them was out of bed. Dawn was right. They didn't want bits and pieces of quality time with Dad ... they wanted quantity. I signed up, attended my first session and began using Sullivan's templates to streamline my business.

I hired an assistant to do my detail and set-up work — someone to handle telephone calls, make appointments, deal with clients in my absence, keep me organized and focused and handle light book-keeping. Before the week began, I would tell my family and clients what days I would work (*focus days*) and which I would play or just hang out with my family (*free days*). I arranged for another realtor to work with my assistant and my clients when I was away on *free days*.

Within the first year, my time with my family increased dramatically. School holidays became *free days* for me and my relationship with my wife and kids blossomed wonderfully. The vast majority of clients respected my new, healthy boundaries. On *focus days*, I felt rested and refreshed and proved remarkably efficient. My income increased substantially. I reveled in my new-found balance.

By now, Dawn and I were the proud parents of three delightful daughters — Juli Ann, Laura Marie and Alana Michelle. I loved and love all three more than words can say. Yet in 1992, when Dawn became pregnant with our fourth child, I found myself yearning for a son. And on March 15, 1993, when the doctor announced, "It's a boy," I just broke down and

41

cried. I was so happy, so elated, so complete. My Lord had answered my prayers and blessed me with a little man child. We christened him Samuel Jess Johnson....

The next three years brought the usual joys and travails of parenthood. By 1996, the four children, ranging in age from three to eight, had begun pestering Dawn and me for cats and dogs and horses and sheep. We adults took a careful look at where we were and, more importantly, where we wanted to be. Our house was paid off, we were financially secure and no longer tied to the city by the requirements of a job. Although I had to be in Edmonton three to five working days each month, what with fax machines, computers, modems and e-mail, we could live anywhere we wanted as long as I could catch a flight to Edmonton without too much difficulty.

The first day we visited Millarville together, exploring the back roads and admiring the mountains, Dawn and I knew without speaking a word to each other that we had found our new community. We proceeded to flaunt our ignorance, however, by asking a local realtor if he could show us some listed acreages. He took a deep breath, ran his fingers through his hair and explained that property in this vicinity didn't list and sell as it did in the city. "It sells like that!" he said, snapping his fingers. "You've got to have an inside track . . . to be in the know."

This didn't surprise me. Being a realtor myself, I understood that he was telling it like it was — that property in Millarville would sell in a heartbeat and no doubt at a premium. Dawn and I set our next goal: "The purchase of a piece of land in Millarville, preferably without a primary residence on it." The time had come to build our dream home. By now, we had seen enough homes, some of them quite glorious, to envisage the place clearly. Undoubtedly, we would go for two stories and strive for both a majestic presence and a rustic feel. The children would have their own bedrooms. The basement would include space for a ping-pong table and a pool table, and a large open kitchen would function as the social centre of the house, the hub around which all else whirled.

This would be our final home — a place where our kids could bring their childhood friends, their boyfriends, their girlfriends . . . their husbands and wives, their children, our grandchildren. More than that, it would serve the family long after Dawn and I were gone. One friend observed that it sounded like we wanted to establish an ancestral home and I realized he was bang on: this would be our legacy to our great great granchildren and their children after them.

As a family, we sat down one Sunday with paper and illustrations to make a collage. We included photos of mountains, of meadows with horses, of a barn with kittens and dogs and kids frolicking about. We taped the finished collage to our "goal wall" (the refrigerator) and invited the universe to weave its magic.

Seven days later, a friend called to say that he had heard of a couple who might be interested in selling their Millarville farm. The following day, I returned to that foothills community, knocked on the door of a cottage on a hill and introduced myself to the somewhat bewildered owners, Bill and Lila. I explained that I'd heard through a friend that they were thinking of selling. After some hesitation, they invited me inside.

Bill and Lila, ranchers at the time, had taken their quarter section (one hundred and sixty acres) on trade in the early 1970s. Each time they came out to visit the property, they found they didn't want to leave. The peace and quiet and sense of community of the surrounding area really grew on them. They spoke of how their kids and grand kids visited. Then Bill admitted: "Well, we've talked about selling. But first we wanted to do some painting and fixing. Anyway, young man, this place is probably not for you. It'll be expensive."

I liked Bill's approach. He wanted to sell but he wasn't going to give anything away, especially not to a young whipper-snapper like myself. I asked the couple if they would show me the property.

Starting high along the eastern boundary, most of it sloped downhill while facing west towards the foothills and the Rockies. It comprised the 800-square-foot log cabin or cottage in which we'd been talking, and that Bill and Lila had built in the late '70s; a Quonset hut with a work bench and room for three vehicles; and a bunk house with a pot-bellied stove. We walked to the apex of the property, which looked out over rolling hills and provided a spectacular view of the Rockies. I asked why they hadn't built their cottage here instead of halfway down the hill among the trees. They said they preferred the shade and protection from the wind.

From the top of the hill, we could see a pond that was roughly the size of a football field and partially surrounded by trees. I tried not to exclaim over its beauty. Bill said he stocked the pond with rainbow trout each spring and enjoyed fishing them out with his kids and grand kids. The longer we spent together, the more I liked Bill and Lila. They were honest, hard-working and placed a heavy emphasis on family.

After the tour and over coffee, I asked them for their best price. Bill looked me in the eye and said, "Well, if I don't have to pay a commission or fix the place up, the price is . . . ." He wrote a number on a scratch pad, then went on: "If you want it, okay. If not, I'll fix it up and list it for a higher price than that. I'm sure someone will pay it."

From the way he spoke, I knew he meant what he said. I also knew he was right: someone would pay more, far more, than the price he had just written down. Meeting that price would be a stretch for Dawn and me, but I knew how perfect this place would be for our family. I knew we could build our dream home here, that Dawn and I could be very comfortable for decades, or at least until we were old, gray and were back in diapers ourselves.

To Bill and Lila, I extended my hand: "You've got a deal."

We wrote and signed an agreement on a piece of scrap paper. It was simple enough, short on legal congestion but solid as the people who signed it. We included the price, the buildings that came with the deal and the possession date. Dawn and I would need to sell our home and make schooling arrangements, but Bill and Lila were flexible, so we agreed to take possession in one year. Driving home to Edmonton, I couldn't wait to see Dawn's face. Our dream was coming true: we were moving to Millarville.

CHAPTER SIX

THE DARKEST NIGHT

Now, as we drove south towards Millarville on the dark night of Sam's passing, Dawn and I took turns making calls. First, I phoned my mother and stepfather. On the third or fourth ring, I looked at the clock on the dashboard and was stunned to realize it was almost three thirty in the morning. On the seventh ring, my mom answered with a tone that suggested she had been asleep for quite a while. I said " Hi, Mom. It's Tim."

Suddenly awake, my Mom cried: "What is it?"

"Mom, is Paul there with you?"

"Yes, he's back in bed."

"Mom, could you get Paul and come back to the telephone?"

She did as I asked and soon they were on different phones.

"Mom, Sam fell into the family pond a little after supper last night...and he drowned. He's dead, Mom."

Three hundred miles away, the impact was devastating.

I said what I could. My mother wanted to keep talking but finally I blurted: "Mom, I've got to go now. We've got to phone other people. I wish the news was better."

"Son, you hang in there."

Dawn's parents were next and the routine repeated itself.

Then we phoned my best friend in Calgary, where he and his wife had joined us at the hospital. He'd worked as a firefighter for the past seventeen years and after I broke the news he replied: "Tim, if it's any consolation, the way Sam died? He felt no pain whatsoever. It's a very calm way to go. You just fall asleep."

We phoned other close friends and family members. Finally we reached a point, just outside the town of Bragg Creek, where the cellular phone no longer worked. We drove into the black night along the deserted, two-lane highway, numb with shock and silent....

When we arrived at the home of the woman who had taken in the children, we found our neighbour sitting up but everyone else fast asleep. As we loaded groggy kids into our car, Juli asked with excited anticipation: "How's Sam? Did you see him? Is he okay?"

"When we get home," I said, "we will tell everybody the news on Sam."

By the time we arrived home, Levi, just eighteen months old, had fallen back to sleep so we tucked him into his crib. Then we brought the three girls to our king-sized bed, which in the short time we'd lived in Millarville had been the site of numerous Wrestlemania battles, fashion shows and rock concerts. There we broke the news that Sam had passed.

Ten-year-old Juli reacted much like Dawn — with shock, disbelief and tears. Laura sat silently in shock. Alana wept softly and pulled the blankets over her head. We talked openly and honestly and encouraged the kids to do the same. It was a hard time. Dawn and I felt self-expression was healthy and important, so we allowed the children to cry, talk and ask questions if they wished. After a long, long time, we began working out sleeping arrangements. The girls all wanted to sleep with Dawn. Even in a king-sized bed, this left little room for me — but to be honest, I wanted to be alone. I went into the bedroom the kids all shared, pulled out the mattress that Sam used as his bed and lay down on it.

That's when I realized, as I lay alone in the darkness: this was it! The dark moment had finally arrived at last — the terrible, dark moment of my recurring premonition. For six years, this moment had haunted me. I would be sitting alone or driving along a lonely highway or even going about my business when suddenly there it would be again, subtly different in shading and yet always the same.

The mood is not black but very grey, cold and murky. My body feels like it's made of lead and weighs five thousands pounds. I can hardly lift my arms. Outside, rain is falling. My surroundings turn surreal. It's like I'm inside a painting by Salvador Dali, but without the whimsy. I feel alone, so alone, and the outlook is bleak and hopeless. There is no one to turn to, no one who can save me. This is not the end of my life, I realize, but a major occurrence in it.

This premonition is not a dream, nor even a day dream, because then you can blink and shake it off, turn your attention to something else. The premonition remains in the air. I can turn my head or go about my daily business but when I look up, there it is again — this suffocating feeling of overwhelming gloom.

The few times I allow the premonition to unfold as completely as possible, I observe that it becomes increasingly difficult to endure — not arithmetically but logarithmically, as with the Richter scale, where each successive digit represents a massive increase in earthquake magnitude. When the premonition comes, I can tolerate it only for the briefest of moments. Yet I try to hang onto it. The longer I hang onto it, the more information it yields — though I pay for any insight with monstrous emotional turmoil.

Venturing into the premonition as far as possible, I have found myself to be about forty years old — an age now just months away. And I've recognized that I'm rocked to the core. I reach out for my wife, for Dawn, and find that I cannot connect with her. She is not within reach. Then I glimpse police officers climbing out of a cruiser. I don't know what the premonition is communicating, but my guess is that it's something about the untimely death of someone extremely dear to me. I can't find Dawn and decide it must be her.

The torment I experience in trying to look further, to venture deeper, is unbearable. I cannot go there, cannot tolerate more, and so I let the premonition go. My intellect dismisses it as silly and then I busy myself, or at least busy my mind.

Now, lying in Sam's bed in Millarville, I realize that the dark moment of the premonition has arrived at last. It is not Dawn I have lost, but Sam! My precious man child! My first begotten son! As the realization settles in, I catch the scent of my Sammy from his pillow, his blankets, and it triggers me. At last the flood gates open and I begin to weep.

I weep for the terror that Sam must have felt as he struggled, cold, wet and frightened. I weep for his loneliness as his cries went unanswered. I weep for the shame I feel over not having been there to protect him, or rescue him, or at least to comfort him. I weep for the loss of my child, a child for whom, as with any of my loved ones, I would have traded my own life in a heartbeat. Finally, I weep for myself. I weep for myself and the despair I feel descending around me like some vast darkness, like some dark night of the soul that threatens to last forever . . . .

CHAPTER SEVEN

HAPPY IN GOD'S COUNTRY

As far as we are concerned, Millarville is God's Country. The values of family and tradition have been driven into the character of this community for more than a century. Millarville boasts a rodeo, a racetrack and a weekly farmers market that attracts people from as far away as Calgary. A typical Saturday morning would find us at that farmers market for breakfast. We would listen to a one-man band playing in the atrium while consuming two Rancher's Specials and four Buckaroos. Then we would ramble around buying tomatoes, carrots, apples, oranges, fresh-made sausage, you name it. We reveled in our new surroundings and proudly showed off a fifth addition to our family, a second son: Levi Jacob Johnson had been born October 20, 1997, just three months after we'd arrived in Millarville.

In July of '97, we had moved into the 800-square foot log cabin on our new quarter-section homestead. This cottage comprised a combined kitchen-living room, two bedrooms, one bathroom and no basement at all. Obviously, squeezing our growing family into that space was a challenge. Dawn and I shared one bedroom, the four older kids shared the other and soon little Levi was sleeping in a crib on the porch. These were tight quarters, but living in the country brought advantages: we could spill outside onto the deck or into the yard or even explore the nearby forest. In the garage side of the Quonset hut, the kids could play hockey or basketball or rollerblade; in the office/bunkhouse side, they could color, play games, surf the net or have sleep-overs.

The log cabin, although quaint, we intended to use only as temporary quarters. We had developed plans to build our dream home higher up on the side of the hill. It would be a two-storey home comprising 10,000 square feet, incorporating stones dug locally and the red cedar that was popular in the area. It would also feature vaulted ceilings and two-storey windows, a couple of turrets and a walkout basement facing the Canadian Rockies.

On April 3, 1998, we started constructing our place in paradise. We told the project manager that we expected workers always to use portable toilets, and that neither foul language nor drinking on site would be tolerated. Since this house was being built for the family, we asked that the children be included and that their questions be answered. We communicated clearly and hired terrific contractors who not only worked skilfully but happily complied. The kids watched the building of the basement, the framing of the walls and the installing of the roof. As the floors went in they picked out their bedrooms and issued stern warnings: "No one allowed in my room without my permission!"

We enjoyed the experience immensely.

Meanwhile, having started school, the kids had been swimming, figure-skating and playing basketball and new friends came quickly. In the city, the children would play for an afternoon; in Millarville, they would almost invariably turn a visit into a sleepover. Much of our introduction to the community came through our children. We got to know the parents of their friends and as the days passed felt more and more at home. We remarked on the sense of community. In the city you can take your neighbor for granted, but in Millarville, folks rely on each other more. You might not always agree with your neighbors, but you always respect them.

Dawn became the president of the early childhood development program (playschool and kindergarten). I volunteered to coach sports and became secretary for the Millarville Sports Association. I was now taking sixteen weeks of *free days* or vacation each year. My income and quality of life continued to appreciate. My relationship with Dawn grew deeper. I felt extremely blessed and gave thanks daily.

Initially, we had hoped to move into our new home by Christmas of 1998. But the local housing market was extremely hot: new-home construction was booming and good workers were in short supply. This slowed building and pushed our possession date to Easter of 1999. No problem. We had grown quite comfortable in the cottage.

Still, as Christmas approached, we faced a decision. Both sets of grandparents lived in or near Wainwright, three hundred miles away. While living in Edmonton, and with most of the children in pre-school, we would spend the major holidays visiting first one side of the extended family, then the other. This year, the older kids had been busy since September with school and at least two extra curricular activities each. The idea of loading up this crew, driving six hours to Wainwright and sleeping in foreign beds for a week proved less than appealing. So, the decision came down from on high: slow down, stay at home and enjoy a lazy holiday with the "Millarvillans."

The run-up to this holiday, which would be our first and last as a family of seven, produced two special adventures — both involving Sam. In one, which centred on finding and decorating the perfect Christmas tree, he played a minor role. As luck would have it, I discovered a secret map that directed us to the perfect tree's precise location. Having donned five sets of jackets, hats and boots and picked up a saw, off we went into the nearby woods.

Here I took the leadership role: "Alana, take twenty-three Minnie Mouse steps due North."

We all followed along until she cried, "Twenty-three, Sir!"

"Laura, take thirty-three and one-half Bugs Bunny steps due West."

Laura, bouncing along, tripped and fell face-first into the snow, cracking everyone up, including herself. Finally, with pronounced buck teeth, paws to her chest and nose twitching, she lisped: "Thirty-three and one half."

"Juli, take twenty-seven Jumbo the Elephant steps North North East."

Juli puts her hands together, sways her arms like an elephant trunk and starts out (everyone else playing along). Rather than verbally indicating completion, she repeatedly stomps her foot and trumpets.

"Sam, take fourteen Superman bounds due East."

Not to be outdone by his sisters, Sam climbs onto a fallen tree and jumps as far as he can: "One." He finds a second tree and repeats this exercise: "Two." Eventually, we arrive at fourteen.

"Okay, the map says to look for the most perfect tree that is about the height of your Dad."

Controversy ensues as each child finds a different tree and claims that it's the perfect specimen. We try presenting arguments but this makes things worse: "My tree is best because . . . ." We try voting but all entries tie at a single vote. While this is happening, I spot a six and a half foot tree that is competing with another, stronger tree and looks likely to wither and die. I rally the troops and begin my own lobbying: "This tree is pretty, it's the right height and it won't live much longer." With that last bit, I win over Juli and Alana, but Laura and Sam remain unconvinced. I convert Laura by drawing her attention to the lovely acorns on the tree and Sam by offering to let him be the first to use the saw

When the tree is cut, the children attack it Three-Stooges style, trying to haul it away in four directions at once. After enjoying this confusion, I suggest they take turns pulling the stump directly towards the house. On arrival, we find that Dawn has prepared hot chocolate and the kids warm their hands on the sides of their mugs. With Dawn's help, I get the tree into the stand and then we two adults sit back and watch while the children do the decorating.

Putting the star on top is still reserved for the youngest member of the family. Juli and Laura lift Levi up into the air. Sam finds the star and gives it to Alana and she hands the star to Levi. After several fumbled attempts, he manages to place it on top. Spontaneous applause breaks out, and Levi claps and smiles the most, all events captured on video. A short while later, when everybody has donned their pajamas and brushed their teeth, Dawn and I read aloud The Night Before Christmas. Kisses and hugs all around, and then we adults announce in unison: "And to all a good night!"

Off they scurry, laughing and squealing, to await Christmas morning.

The second holiday adventure in which Sam played a major role had begun at a Canadian Tire store in Calgary. I had brought five-year-old Sam along while I was picking up outdoor lights, wrapping paper and a new snow shovel. In the store, Sam asked if I would buy "the family," as he put it, a toboggan he coveted. I had already bought and hidden two toboggans for "the family" and needed a reason to hold him off: "Sam, I'm not going to buy a toboggan right now. It's too early in the season. There's no snow on the ground."

Without hesitation, Sam said: "Then why are you buying a new snow shovel?"

It was as if, without quite realizing it, I'd started playing a game of chess with Sam and he'd just embarrassed me badly by taking my queen on his third move. Like all our children, Sam was sharp, and with each passing day, was becoming harder to fend off with lame excuses. To distract him while I regrouped, I said: "Tell me the one thing you want, more than anything else, for Christmas! Take your time and think about it."

We cleared the till, loaded the Suburban and began the drive home. Sam, having deliberated carefully, and plotting each move like a champion chess player, arrived at the single thing he wanted: "The one thing I want for Christmas, Dad, is a motorcycle — a blue, fast, very cool motorcycle." He said this sternly, his brow furrowed, and in a tone that implied: "I not only want this, but expect it."

I measured my words: "Sam, you're simply too young for a motorcycle."

Sam spent the next few minutes justifying his position. "I'll be careful…other kids have them… I'll be very, very good." He noticed he wasn't getting anywhere and assumed more of a victim position: "If you don't give me a motorcycle, I'll take your car keys. I'll hide your wallet. I'll tell your mom on you!" In an attempt to be compassionate, I made another bad move: "Sam, winter is coming. Even if Santa gave you a motorcycle, you couldn't ride it until spring. Besides, you would have to share it with all your siblings!"

By now, Sam's mental computer was processing information at warp speed. Immediately, he spotted the weakness in my defence. But instead of moving too fast, he backed off and lulled me into a false sense of security: "I'll share it Dad, honest. But never mind. You and Mom can wait until my birthday next spring to give me a motorcycle."

Sam paused and I thought I'd won. I lost focus and allowed my mind to wander, but then he made his next move, and I grasped the situation: I was a novice chess player and he was Bobby Fischer disguised as a five-year-old. "Dad, if I can have only one thing for Christmas," he said, "then I want a skidoo! A blue, very cool, small, just-for-kids, skidoo. And I'll share it with all my sisters and Levi, too!"

Check! My king was in serious trouble. I flashed back to my own childhood, wondering how my father would have dealt with this situation. He would have bellowed, "You'll take what I give you and bloody well be happy with it!" I let that option pass, took a deep breath and softly said, "Son, neither Santa, Mom nor I will even consider giving you, or anyone else in this family, a motorcycle, a skidoo, or anything else motorized until you're at least twelve years old. That's just the way it is."

To Sam, it must have felt like I'd cleared the chess board with a swift backhand. He was deflated and sullen as we pulled into the driveway. I sensed he needed comforting so I went to the passenger side and offered him a piggyback ride to the house. Offering him my hands as stirrups, I started off walking but he gave me the spurs and I broke into a canter, pulling up just short of the porch. After considerable snorting and whinnying, I bent down to allow a smooth dismount.

Sam sat down on the step and, almost inaudibly, said: "Dad?"

I sat down beside him: "Yeah, little buddy?"

In a soft, deliberate voice, Sam said: "What I really want for Christmas, more than anything else . . . is to be twelve years old."

Sam took off his shoes and quietly entered the cottage.

Checkmate!

CHAPTER EIGHT

AT THE POND

The first morning after Sam's death, having slept not at all, I rolled out of bed early. I looked into our master bedroom and saw that everyone else was still slumbering. Grief was calling me but I pushed it away: work had to be done. Arrangements had to be made, an obituary had to be written, people would be stopping by to give their condolences.

I went outside and moved our vehicles out of the main driveway. I took the recycle materials off the porch and put them in the shed. I did my best to make the place look presentable. The telephone started ringing at six-thirty (it wouldn't stop until well after eleven o'clock that night). At times like these, people often say the same things: "Oh my God, Tim! We just heard about it, we're devastated, we're so sorry for you guys. What can we do? Anything, anything at all, just call. I know you probably can't talk right now, but we'll drop off something. Let us know, just let us know."

Meanwhile, Dawn joined me. Quietly, working together, knowing each others's movements, we straightened the house and made it ready for well-wishers. Just before 7:00 a.m., an RCMP cruiser pulled into our yard. Two officers emerged from the vehicle, one on each side. Looking out, I recognized the scene — and suddenly felt stunned beyond belief. This was it! The scene I had glimpsed, repeatedly, in my premonition. As the two RCMP officers approached, the enormity of this coincidence overwhelmed me. I broke down completely. Now I understood why I had never been able to hold onto this premonition: the gravity of the real-life event turned me to absolute jello.

Once I had collected myself, Dawn and I and the two RCMP officers, a sergeant and a constable, sat on the edge of the porch. Still no one had spoken — not a single word. Finally, the sergeant began, observing that "Robert," the caregiver's husband, had risked his life three times trying to get to Sam: "Everyone did their very best . . . Tim and Dawn, I'm truly sorry."

I nodded, not trusting myself to speak.

Into the silence, the sergeant said: "Are you satisfied with how everything went?"

This was the heaviest question yet. Every word the sergeant spoke, every second of silence, carried a terrible weight. The RCMP officer's question was simple and concise yet freighted with a million subtleties and implications. I did not need an interpreter to understand its dreadful gravity. This was the turning point in the RCMP investigation. The sergeant was asking: Are these parents angry? Are they looking for someone to blame?

Despite the state I was in, I knew that the next words out of my mouth would be critical. Barbara was a good and diligent caregiver — fair, compassionate and attentive to our children's needs. Had she made a mistake the previous day in caring for Sam? The quote that rings true for me comes from the Book of Matthew: "Judge not, that ye be not judged. For with what judgment ye judge, ye shall be judged . . . ."

Both Barbara and Robert had done their best to save Sam. I know Sam would have heard Robert and realized the man was doing his best to reach him, to save him. This was a modern-day tragedy of epic proportions. Dawn and I looked at each other, both of us recognizing this turning point for what it was. We hadn't discussed it, but really we didn't need to: we knew each other that well. The RCMP needed clarification, however, and I delivered it as clearly and succinctly as I could: "Everyone had a part to play . . . and no one is to blame."

The RCMP officers didn't exhale, exactly. Rather, it was like they began breathing for the first time since they arrived. Dawn and I felt as if we had thrown off a great weight. We couldn't have articulated it at the time, but we had chosen our path. We had resolved, and we had announced our resolve, to move in one direction and not another — to shun blaming and retribution and move towards healing and spiritual growth and development. We appreciated the rescue efforts, which had been flawless in their execution, and admired all those who had made them. We had no intention of pursuing charges against anyone... nobody was to blame.

The RCMP officers, visibly relieved, paid their condolences and departed.

Soon friends and relations began arriving, people bringing flowers, salads, casseroles, whole meals — and thank God they did. People saying, "Here, here's some casserole, I just warmed it up, you should eat it. Here's a glass of water, you should really go lie down. Are you okay? Do you want to talk?"

The support was tremendous. Dawn and I both cherished it immensely, and yet . . . to tell the truth, on some level it made no difference. The hurt, the pain, the reality of my loss began to overwhelm me. As the day wore on, I did my best to touch, hold, kiss and caress my wife and children — to remain as open as I possibly could to them.

Evening came and, for the first time since my

son's death, I walked the half kilometer down the road to the pond where Sam had spent his last moments on this planet. The pond is about the size and shape of a football field with end zones at north and south. Arriving on the east side, nearest the house, I registered but paid little attention to a small, greying, wooden cross that stood at water's edge, and against which fishermen had leaned their rods. Later, a visitor would call my attention to the premonitory symbolism of this worn wooden cross, which had sat at the edge of the pond since before Sam was born, and which now marked the spot where most likely he had ventured onto the ice.

The ice on the east side was maybe three inches thick and still strong — strong enough, certainly, to hold Sam, and probably strong enough even to hold me. But if a person started across the pond toward the ice-bound dock, he would find the ice growing thin and slick with a layer of water. The wind had been whipping at the pond for days. On the west side, the ice gave way to open water. Clearly, the closer a person came to that open water, even a young person of fifty pounds, the more danger he faced. I stood on the shore trying to get inside Sam's head. Why would he go onto the pond? We'd warned them all so many times. We'd even driven them down here specifically to tell them it was dangerous. What would possess him? What would lure him? What would drive him towards the ice-bound dock?

I remembered late last spring. On the floating dock, inside a large truck tire, a Canada goose had laid five perfect eggs. I'd taken the kids out one by one in our twelve-foot rowboat and told them they could look at the eggs but couldn't touch them, that otherwise their human scent might drive away the mother. Each child, Sam included, looked on in wonder. I thought: did Sam go out to look for goose eggs? Even though he'd been warned against that?

I remembered last November, how as winter came on, the ice on the pond began to freeze over. Just before Christmas the ice looked thick enough to carry the combined weight of the Johnson family. More than once, I told Dawn to keep an eye on me from the house. Then I would go down to the pond and lay two eight-foot two-by-fours on the outside edge of the ice, to distribute my weight. I would get down on my hands and knees and, with my cordless drill, auger a hole in the ice six inches deep: here, at least, the ice was thick enough to carry a truck. I would crawl out another ten feet and, using my trusty two-by-fours, augur another hole. The new ice cracked, pinged and complained under my weight, but finally I found ice six inches thick at the middle of the pond. I stood up, walked back to shore and started tightening up five sets of skates — four for the kids and one for me.

All of the children enjoyed skating, but Sam absolutely loved it. On weekdays, I would manage to hold him off until three in the afternoon. Then I would load skates, hockey sticks, a tennis ball and a net into the back of our pick-up truck and drive down to the pond. As soon as I laced up Sammy's skates, he was gone. At three-fifteen the school bus would pull up at our gate beside the blue teepee I had built as a bus shelter for the children. The arriving girls would run, squealing, all the way to the pond (a distance of about one hundred yards) and lace on their skates. Sometimes they would play hockey with Sam and me. Sometimes they'd skate on their own. Sometimes we'd all play tag, Red Rover or British Bulldog. Always we had a wonderful time.

I'm not sure how it started, but when Sam and I played hockey, I would do a running commentary like the ones Danny Gallivan and Dick Irvine used to do on Hockey Night in Canada: "Good evening, everybody. Here we are at the Forum in Montreal where the visiting Edmonton Oilers are about to do battle with the Montreal Canadians. The story that's all the buzz around the forum, as well as the rest of the hockey world, is the recent emergence of the young superstar Sam Johnson, who is only five years old. Sam was playing in relative obscurity on a pond in Millarville, Alberta, when the wiley Oilers G.M., Glen Sather, scouted and signed him as a free agent.

"Sam reported to the Cape Breton Oilers where he quickly ran up some impressive figures, counting fourteen goals and seventeen assists in the first three games of the season. Meanwhile, injuries have left Wayne Gretzky short of a line-mate to capitalize on his picture-perfect passing, so young Sam Johnson was called up and here he is today, playing in his very first National Hockey League game. Now, since Sam is three feet seven inches tall and weighs only forty-seven pounds soaking wet, the National Hockey League has adopted a policy of no hitting. The players are not allowed any physical contact — not only against Wayne Gretzky, the Oilers captain, but also against his new sidekick, Sam Johnson."

At this point, I would skate over to Sam and pretend I had a microphone in my hand: "Sam, tell the National Hockey League audience here today how you feel."

He would say something real catchy, like: "Good."

"Sam, we understand that you are here to burn up the league, set a new bench mark for goal production and perhaps win the Calder Trophy as the league's top rookie. Is there anything that you would like to say to our viewing audience?"

Sam would look at me and say, "Dad, I like it when you do the voice thing, but I don't want to talk, I just want to play hockey."

Off we'd go. I was expected not only to feed Sam the puck perfectly, like Wayne Gretzky, but also to do the play-by-play of Danny Gallivan and the color commentary of Dick Irvine. "Gretzky gobbles up the puck. He's moving up the ice. Sam Johnson's in front of the net, he's got himself set up. Gretzky feathers the puck over and Sam one times it . . . he scores!!!" Sam would throw his arms in the air and skate around the pond a couple of times. He really ate it up. We would carry on with this running commentary for a time, but then I'd get tired of doing the routine and we would settle down to just playing hockey.

Sam would have played all day long. He couldn't get enough. Whether we played basketball, baseball, Wrestlemania or hockey, he was the same. He would play and play and play and play. And if not for the complaining of one of the girls about being tired, being cold or having sore feet from where the skates were too tight, probably we would have played until dark. Dawn used to say that Sam would rather play sports than eat — and he loved to eat.

In any event, the scene repeated itself over and over again that winter. Sam would come home from school, we'd eat lunch and do odd jobs around the house, and then a little after three p.m., we would head down to the pond with our sticks, gloves and skates and away we'd go.

So it went until mid-March. Then one Saturday morning, I got up and looked west towards the Rockies and saw a Chinook arch forming in the sky — a friendly reminder that a warm strong wind would soon descend upon us. I rousted the kids and asked them if they wanted to go for "the last skating party of the year." I knew that, with the warming trend we had been experiencing, the ice on our pond would not last a lot longer. Once the six-inch thickness was gone, I would deem it unsafe.

So after some coaxing and gathering of equipment, the kids and I headed down to the pond.

We all played hockey for a while and then the girls decided to play frozen tag. Sam and I continued our game. We knew each other, anticipated each other's movements like a couple who had danced together all their lives. I could sense, without looking, where he was, and softly lay the tennis ball on his stick in good position for him to shoot. He would then fish the ball out of the goal and roll it towards the corner, knowing I would soon turn into its path. Then he would circle the net, as if to cut off a would-be checker, as I had taught him, before moving back into position to "one-time" the ball I returned to him. A smile or a nod replaced the enthusiastic commentary.

Inevitably, on the day I didn't want to end, one of the kids started complaining about feet. We gathered up the sticks, pucks, nets and skates and loaded everything into the back of the pick-up. A tennis ball remained unaccounted for, but after Sam and I had searched for a while, we decided to look again in the spring, when inevitably it would float ashore.

Before climbing back into the truck, I said, "Listen, gangsters. I need everybody's attention." After some good natured chirping, the kids noticed the stern look on my face and fell silent. I said: "Do you see the water that is starting to form on the west side of the pond? How there's a thin layer of water on top of the ice?"

"Yes, Dad, we can see that."

"That water tells you that the pond is no longer safe — that the ice is getting thinner and turning into water. So, this is the last time we are going to skate on the pond this year. Pretty soon the ice will not be strong enough to support us and the last thing we want is anyone falling through the ice, right? So the pond is now off limits. I don't want anybody on the ice. Does everybody understand?"

They all nodded their heads solemnly. I looked at Juli: "What do you understand, Juli?"

"Dad, I understand that the ice is melting. If we try to go for a skate on it, we might fall in."

"Yes, that's right. And because of that, we can't go on the ice any more."

We all jumped into the vehicle and headed up the hill.

The next day was Sunday. We had long been in the habit of going out for Sunday dinner and, late in the afternoon, we began preparing to drive into the nearby town of Bragg Creek. We herded the kids into the family vehicle, strapped Levi into his child seat and drove down the long driveway. Just before turning onto the highway, Dawn looked out and said, "Tim, we should talk to the kids about the pond."

"Dawn, I did that yesterday. But, you know, let's do it again."

I turned the car around and drove down the road to the fence around the pond, pulling up a few feet from the water. I said, "Now listen, kids. I've got something to tell you."

Laura said saucily: "What are you going to tell us this time, Dad?"

"Laura, this is serious. I want you to listen. The pond is no longer safe. You guys can not walk on the pond anymore. There's a good chance that anybody going on the pond might fall through. So it's off limits."

Alana said, "Dad, you told us this yesterday!"

"Yes, Alana, I know. I just want you all to be clear." Then I said, "Sam, tell me what I just told you."

He said, "Not to go on the pond."

"That's right, Sam. Okay, let's go for supper!"

Now, as I stood gazing, broken-hearted, at the pond where Sam had spent his last moments, I found myself wondering: Had he perhaps seen a hockey puck out on the pond? Had he walked out across the thick ice to pick up that puck? When he got there, did he maybe see a tennis ball a little farther out, and venture out onto the thinner ice to retrieve it? I found it very difficult to look at the ice that had been broken during the rescue. Yet as difficult as it was, I felt a deep curiosity. I wanted to know: what was it like for Sam in those final moments?

I took off my shoes and socks, rolled up my pant legs and stepped carefully into the unbelievably frigid water. Immediately, my muscles began to ache ferociously. I got a flash of the movie Titanic, remembered Leonardo DeCaprio at the stern of the ship describing what it's like diving into frigid water, saying to Kate Winslet: "It hits you like a thousand knives stabbing you all over your body. You can't breathe, you can't think…at least not about anything but the pain."

As I stood aching in the water, I realized that, even though Sam had been growing like a bad weed, he remained a skinny, fifty-pound, six-year-old: he could not have lasted long in water this cold. Water just above freezing — barely zero degrees Celsius — would have sucked the life right out of his body.

I stepped out of the water, put my shoes back on and walked around to the west side of the pond, where the water lay open, free of ice. I tried to formulate scenarios that would reverse this tragedy. Why couldn't I have been here that day? Why couldn't I have arrived ten seconds after he fell in? Why couldn't I have paid attention to those feelings, those intuitions I'd experienced? Why didn't I get into my vehicle and drive home from Banff?

Arriving, perhaps I would have seen him on the dock, maybe still looking for a tennis ball or walking on the ice. Maybe he would have felt embarrassed that I had seen him, but perhaps I could have driven over and said, "Sam, stay there! Don't move a muscle until we can get to you." Perhaps I would have seen him fall in. Perhaps I would have seen him in the water, and would have raced around to the west side and plunged into the water and swam out to him and pulled him back to shore, back to safety....

I stood a long time, looking out at the pond. Then, slowly, I walked back up the steep driveway to our home. I slipped quietly into our bedroom and closed the door. There were fifteen, maybe twenty people in our small residence, and I knew that our remaining children were being cared for. I just needed some time alone, some time to grieve, some time to cry.

That night I stayed up late, talking with Dawn and some other family members, mostly just pondering what the hell it was that was going on in my life. What had I done to anger my God or the Universe so much, that I was being punished this way? Was there any message to be found in this ocean of grief?

CHAPTER NINE

SPY VERSUS SPY

I've mentioned how, until I did some intense personal work, I paid little attention to my intuition. Certainly, I didn't imagine that intuition could play a role in the way I live — or even the size of my family. The birth of Sam in 1993 provided one of the great highs of my life, yet it came during a particularly difficult time. Using the Dan Sullivan "Coach" Program, I'd created *free days* for the first time in my life; but some of those days, I didn't like who I saw in the mirror. My upbringing had been dysfunctional. My father was a raving, cruel drunk with a caustic tongue who often left me stinging from his sharp criticisms. My mother, in contrast, was doting and co-dependant. They had a passive/aggressive relationship that I hated, despised and promised myself I would never adopt.

Shortly after Sam's birth, I found myself languishing in the lowest of lows. I was working far too hard and suffering from sleep deprivation, which is guaranteed to magnify any problems. More and more often, Dawn and I found ourselves acting out negative programming we had learned from our parents. To put it plainly, our marriage was failing. I've always believed that the quality of my life was based on the questions I was willing to ask myself. To use the current vernacular, the quality of my life sucked — it sucked big time.

At my lowest point I turned to a friend. I spilled my guts, gave him a Reader's Digest version of my current situation, and he told me about a program that might help. Late that day, I phoned and booked myself into a nine-day personal development program called the Hoffman Process. The Hoffman Process is an extended, intensive, non-denominational workshop led by highly skilled teachers in a dormitory environment. Initially, it places a strong emphasis on disconnecting from negative patterns adopted by mother and father. This cathartic work is performed in numerous ways, including pillow pounding.

Then comes defence work for mother and father — exploring why they did what they did. The process is experiential. To me that means different people get different things out of it. Once I had completed about eighty per cent of the program, the facilitator introduced an exercise called "The Symbol Trip." It began with quieting the chattering monkeys. My experience of the chattering monkeys is that they are really my own intellect and emotions doing continuous battle. My intellect says, "Let's be logical, this has to make sense." My emotions say, "No, I'm frightened," or "Let's have fun!" It's a classic push-pull conflict that reminds me of those Spy-Versus-Spy cartoons in Mad Magazine, in which each spy is constantly trying to conquer and control the other. Quieting these monkeys is vital because once they are still, my mind becomes clear and calm and then I can move on.

The next part of the exercise involved posing a question on the premise that the answers to all of life's questions reside within me. So, I asked: "How can I have a closer, more meaningful relationship with my wife and children?" Then I closed my eyes and held my right hand open in front of my heart, allowing a symbol to appear. To my surprise (in my mind's eye), a picnic table appeared. I wondered if I had done this wrong, so I repeated the exercise. Again, a picnic table appeared. I was assured that I should trust the symbol: its meaning would come to me in due course.

The last few days of the Hoffman Process are devoted to reintegrating all the tools and aspects of the process. I spent those days, for the first time in my life, with a new-found sense of peace and groundedness. Over the nine days I gained numerous things. I gained compassion, instead of contempt, for my mother and father, and tools to deal with both my overt and covert anger. I also gained a profound sense of inner peace, insight into my intuition and how to tap into it, a deep inner sense of awareness... but most importantly, I gained back my life.

I returned home, swept up my wife and children and hugged them like I had never hugged them before. I continued to do my work as issues came up, but I knew I had turned a vital corner in my life. My first night home, Dawn said, "You know how the kids love to play on the jungle gym you built in the back yard? Well, why not build a picnic table beside the jungle gym so we can sit and visit while the kids play?"

Bingo! the symbol trip did work! The next day I bought the lumber and crafted a picnic table. Ever since, the picnic table has served as a frequent place to sit with a coffee and enjoy the kids, sharing the day's events or gathering for a picnic or birthday party. It truly has facilitated a closer relationship with my wife and kids.

My close friends noticed a change. My children noticed a change. And Dawn, after waiting a few months to see if the change would wear off, accepted the transformation as permanent. In September of 1993, she took the Hoffman Process herself. Eventually, Dawn completed the rigorous training required and became a certified Hoffman facilitator.

I can honestly say that, without a doubt, had Dawn and I not found this program, done our work to make a shift and recommitted to ourselves and each other, we would not be together today. Worse, we would have probably have entered right back into similar, if not identical, relationships, and in so doing, passed on our learned negative patterns and behaviours to our children. One quote that rings true for me is: "Life keeps giving the same test until you pass it." Dawn and I passed the test and a new world opened up for us. My life took on a new depth and texture — and also I noticed a few other, not so predictable, changes.

After my personal work, I began to tap into a source inside me that was neither intellect nor emotion, but rather intuition — a knowing, something beyond the five senses. A couple of years before, my daughter Alana and I had spent important bonding time at Disneyworld. She was only four months old and I was the one who, for eight days, carried her around in a snuggly, her little face right up close to mine. Now she was four. We would walk in the park and, from time to time — not always, but whenever I could clear my mind and silence the chattering monkeys — Alana and I, with no conscious effort, would share thoughts without speaking a word.

The first few times this happened, I brushed it off as silly, my intellect discounting the experience as a coincidence. But that atttitude changed forever one day. Four-year-old Alana and I were walking along hand in hand, each in a separate world — or so I thought. Some Canada geese flew overhead and I thought how wonderful it must be to fly like a bird and how much I would like to be one. Alana piped up: "Not me, Dad. I want to be the sky, big and blue, so I can see everything and everybody."

I stopped, knelt down on one knee and looked her in the eye. "Alana, why did you say that?"

"Cause of what you said about the gooses, Dad."

I knew I hadn't said say anything out loud, but also realized that if I made too big a deal out of this, Alana might shut down. So I stood up and we continued walking hand in hand, sharing what we really wanted to be, the sky or geese....

Many, many times since then, Alana and I have shared thoughts and feelings without uttering a word. I remember the afternoon of "the dancing pink dress." I had arrived home early one afternoon after a horrible day. This was when we still lived in Edmonton. I had been wrapped up in my work, struggling to get people to see things my way, until finally everything had blown up in my face. I decided that the real problem was not everyone else... it was me. Tired and frustrated, I slumped into my car and drove home.

I walked into the front room, grabbed a pillow, turned on some easy listening music and lay down in the middle of the floor to unwind. Ester, our nanny, was busy at work and the only other person in the house was Alana. She was clad in a white T-shirt and blue jeans and was sitting at the dinner table, coloring. With my eyes closed I asked the universe to sooth me, guide me...help me out! Soon after my silent request, Alana went upstairs and returned wearing her pink Cinderella dress. She danced and danced and danced all around me.

As I watched her twirl and pirouette around and around, tears began rolling down my face. I have no idea how long Alana danced. I lost track of time. Eventually, however, she came over and laid down beside me with her head on my arm and whispered,

"Dad, I love you".

It was so magical, so profound, and all so very simple.

Often when I let go, clear my mind and allow myself to "be clean," to exist totally in the moment, important insights come to me. I think of these intuitive moments as *Being Clean* and during them I experience a wonderful sense of peace, calm and tranquility. Not all communications are simple. Sometimes I receive information over time.

Out walking one day, I posed the question, "How can I be a better father?"

At that instant, fifty yards in front of me, seven geese honked and flew past. In my psychologically open state, I found this perplexing. What did these geese mean? What did they have to do with my question? My intellect promptly responded: nothing. It's just a coincidence. I resumed walking: perhaps the universe would get back to me at a later date.

The following week, business took me to Vancouver, British Columbia. I had a couple of hours between meetings so I went for a walk in Stanley Park. I was enjoying a moment of *Being Clean* when two huge Canada Geese banked not ten feet in front of me and landed on a pond immediately to my left. This natural event arrested my attention. I stood and watched the two majestic geese paddle about the pond.

As I stood there, lost in another world, four more Canada geese began their descent into the pond, so close over my head that I could feel their breeze. For the longest time, I watched the flock swim, dive and establish pecking order. Then, out of nowhere, a lone gosling swooped in, making a perfect two-point landing, and bringing the total to seven. A glow filled me as I returned to the hotel. I didn't know what the geese meant, if anything, but I liked having them around.

That night at my evening meeting, out of the blue, a client to whom I had never spoken of geese handed me a piece of paper. She said, "I saw this and thought you might like a copy."

THE GOOSE STORY

Next fall, when you see geese heading south for the winter...flying along in 'V' formation...you might consider what science has discovered as to why they fly that way.

As each bird flaps its wings, it creates an uplift for the bird immediately following. By flying in 'V' formation, the whole flock adds at least 71 per cent greater flying range than if each bird flew on its own.

When a goose falls out of formation, it suddenly feels the drag and resistance of trying to go it alone...and quickly gets back into the formation to take advantage of the lifting power of the bird in front.

When the head goose gets tired, it rotates back in the wings and another goose flies point. Geese honk from behind to encourage those up front to keep up their speed.

Finally, and this is important...when a goose gets sick, or is wounded by gunshots, and falls out of formation, two other geese fall out of formation and follow him down to help and protect him.

They stay with the fallen goose until it is able to fly again, or until it dies, and only then do they launch out on their own or with another formation to catch up with their group.

The symbols I receive when I'm *Being Clean* are always simple — like a flock of geese. Their meaning, however, is usually profound. Each time I read the Goose Story, or observe this majestic bird in nature, I get a different piece of information about loyalty, sticking together or how to be a better person, a better husband, a better father.

But what of the seven geese? In 1993, after the birth of Sam, Dawn, myself and four kids made only six. On the home front, Dawn and I were enjoying our relationship in new ways. Saturday night, we would hire a sitter and go out on the town — sometimes to a special event, other times just for pizza and a movie. I was falling in love with Dawn all over again. That was when it hit me: I had a moment of clarity and realized: I want another child.

I shared this notion with a close friend who said, "Buy a dog."

No, no… that wouldn't do. I wanted another child. But I felt Dawn would be averse to the idea. Even though we would share in many of the parenting duties, she would still have to deal with pregnancy, putting on weight, diapers, feedings, no sleep. I found myself remembering Sam as a baby, and specifically awakening one night to his fussing.

I looked at the clock, it was three something a.m. As I rolled over to get up, Dawn moaned, "I'll get him." Dawn had seen such a profound change in our relationship that she had recently started the rigorous training to become a certified Hoffman facilitator. Tomorrow morning, she would be on the bird to Toronto for nine days. She would make this trip ten times in the next year, finally to become a full-fledged facilitator. As the mother of four, she described the Toronto flight as "four hours of quiet time with great service and a movie." Perhaps for the chance to tend to her son one last time before she left, she got up.

After a while, I could still hear Sam fussing. His fussing got louder, then quieter, then louder again, then quieter. The fussing escalated to crying . . . then panic. I jumped out of bed, pulled on my robe and stumbled out into the hallway. Dawn was holding Sam in his blanket, staggering down the hallway, patting him on the back, trying to sooth him. It wasn't until she turned around at the far end of the hallway, and started coming back towards me, that I realized why Sam was so distressed: Dawn was holding him upside down.

"Dawn," I said wryly. "Try turning him over."

In her sleep-deprived state, she looked down and then: "Oh, my God!"

She flipped him over and hugged him tightly to her chest, repeating over and over, "Sammy, I'm so, so sorry . . . Sammy, I'm so sorry." I knew Dawn would stay with Sam now until he fell back to sleep. So, just for fun, I pulled all our blankets off, put the pillows at the foot of our bed and made the bed "upside down." When Dawn finally returned, she stared at the arrangement, puzzled, and then, in a mock huff, crawled into bed beside me....

Four years later, such memories continued to flood me, feeding my yearning for yet another child. Finally, I shared my desire with Dawn. To my surprise, she had been thinking the very same thing. We idealistically thought: this could be our love child, a child conceived and reared with new-found awareness and in unconditional love — without much of the garbage we had been carrying from our childhoods and which we'd inflicted, in some ways, on our first four children.

I was elated. Dawn was elated. So what next?

We faced one major hurdle. Shortly after the birth of Sam, I had undergone a vasectomy. Although in the early days, Dawn and I had talked of having as many as six children, the reality was we both felt "stretched to the max" with four. And so it happened that, after visiting the doctor one day, I limped home and didn't move for the entire weekend. I said to Dawn (in between moans) "This must be what it feels like after you give birth right?"

"Yes, Tim, I'm sure the experience is identical."

So: my plumbing had been capped. Could it be uncapped??

Off to the urologist I went. After a brief examination, he said he could perform the "reversal" and described the procedure as a "delicate micro-surgical procedure with a high probability for success." Before I laid my "ahoms" on the line, I asked if he could upgrade the probability to one hundred per cent and, for the sake of my ego, refer to the procedure as "Macro." He politely and professionally reiterated his original line.

The thought of fathering one last child was so alluring that I went ahead. Within a few days of the procedure I turned from a limping, slow-moving behemoth into a snorting, rutting bull moose! Dawn and I had always enjoyed a healthy love life but this was like a couple of kids with a new toy. Then, like clockwork, Dawn announced she would be delivering our fifth child sometime in mid-October of 1997. I asked when she had seen the doctor. She just smiled and said, "I haven't seen the doctor, I just know!"

The birth of our fifth child turned into something quite special. We had asked our children if they wanted to be present for the birth and they all said yes. We found a doctor who was open to the idea of having not just myself and my wife in the delivery room but our four young children as well. We talked to our children about what to expect and what they might see. Mom might struggle and be in some pain, but she would be okay. Then early one morning in October, we packed our sleepy-eyed, pajama-clad clan into our suburban and off to the hospital we went.

With Teddy bears, pillows, blankets and kids in tow, Dawn arrived at the hospital. While she looked after the business at hand, I bedded down the kids in the waiting room where they could snooze until the final moments of delivery. When Dawn was fully dilated and started to give birth, I rousted the kids and ushered them into the delivery room. The look on their faces was unbelievable. They were not frightened, they were not concerned, they were there, fully in the moment, captivated by the miracle at hand. Finally, after nine months and much ado, at seven fifty-seven in the morning of October 20, 1997, weighing in at eight pounds four ounces, Levi Jacob Johnson entered the world.

The next few days, the kids had this incredible glow about them. The experience was extremely positive, not only for Dawn, myself and Levi, but also for Juli, Laura, Alana and Sam. They had just experienced a unique, transformative event and their faces showed it. We had a special child welcomed into the world by our entire family. We felt blessed and honored to be bringing him home — a second son.

CHAPTER TEN

SUPER SAM JOHNSON

I lay on the couch for a while, probably slept a bit but soon it was morning. The house was quiet. This was the day I was going to the city to make arrangements for the cremation of my son's body. I left a quiet house and drove the three miles to the home of Dwight Weinberger, a friend I'd known since high school. Dwight had volunteered to drive me to the crematorium, where we would be joined by Brent Wanvig. Brent and I had met in grade four and had been best friends ever since. Both men, ironically, had become Calgary fire fighters — the kind of guys who show up when there's a tough job to do and stay until it's finished. Having the two of them present meant a lot to me.

At the crematorium, I signed papers and picked out an urn for Sam's ashes. A patient, considerate attendant then asked which type of coffin I would like for the cremation. The word "coffin" seemed weighted with lead, it struck me that bluntly. I knew my son had passed away but "coffin" was so final... my heart sank another fathom.

The attendant showed me several options, including a basic pine box: "Keeping in mind that it is going to be cremated immediately after your son is placed in it," he said, "you might want to consider this."

The box was roughly finished and had yellow nylon ropes for handles. I knew it made economic sense, but I didn't want that for my son. I asked if he had something that was finished, with a pillow and some soft lining, so Sam could be comfortable. Most of the caskets were full size (for adults), but he did have access to one model, both finished and with a pillow, in the appropriate size. As he described and showed its features, I felt more at ease. I sensed it was right but couldn't speak, so I nodded my approval. As the attendant filled out the order, I noticed the name of the model: "Mother Goose."

Once again, the image of a goose or geese followed me and my family.

Outside the crematorium, I thanked Brent for coming and waved goodbye. Dwight and I climbed into the car and headed south through Calgary towards Millarville. Feeling thirsty, I asked Dwight to stop at a convenience store. I took one step inside and was frozen in my tracks. The front page of every newspaper in the rack was filled with a photograph of my son's smiling face. Someone had given the media an image of Sam, and the stark reality of it caught me completely off guard.

As I gawked at the images of my son, grief welled up inside me. I grappled with it unsuccessfully and, just before I completely broke down, stumbled out the door and ran back to the car empty-handed. I stood leaning over the roof of the car, my face in my hands, sobbing, as I struggled to come to terms with the pain of Sam's loss.

All the the way home, I kept thinking that this was not a bad dream that was going to go away. This was real. The cold, stark, icy reality was setting in. I also realized that making the arrangements, driving into the city, talking with Dwight — all these were partial escapes. I was looking for somwhere to hide so I wouldn't have to confront my own grief.

Encountering Sam's image in the convenience store had given me a brief look at how vast that grief was, and how daunting the task of coming to terms with it would be.

I struggled through the rest of the day. The pastor came over and we discussed an finalized the service, many details of which I had not even considered. Around ten o'clock that night, I sat down with Dawn and started to rough out a eulogy for our son. This dredged up all kinds of memories and at one point I found myself reminiscing about a trip Sam and I had made to Vanouver the previous spring.

A good friend had called to inform me that the National Hockey League All-Star Game was being held in that West Coast city. He had two tickets, was unable to attend, and could I use them? I talked with Dawn, consulted my schedule and then claimed the tickets. The thought of a father-son All-Star weekend in Vancouver made me downright giddy so I sprang it on the boy. He became so excited about the idea that he immediately started packing his bags. For the next three weeks, Sam would ask several times a day, "Are we going tomorrow, Dad?"

Finally, the big day arrived. We drove into Calgary and boarded the plane. Family outings are always a pleasure, but "one on one" outings, like this one with Sam, always take on a different dimension. In these situations, with any of my children, I notice that an ease develops, a kinship that is warm and wonderful and loving. Perhaps it's because they receive my undivided attention and do not have to compete with their siblings.

At the Vancouver terminal, our luggage in hand, I asked Sam if he would prefer to take a cab to the hotel or…a "limo." Sam jumped into the limo, opened the sunroof, turned up the stereo and poked his head through the sunroof. He entertained me all the way to the hotel, simply by acting just like a five-year-old.

We had no sooner settled into a room overlooking Granville Island than a pillow fight broke out and quickly escalated into a full-blown, Wrestlemania grudge-match. True to my newly created villain-character, The Eliminator, I used every dirty trick I knew to gain an unfair advantage over Super Sam. Super Sam was a character that drew on Superman's best attributes while adding copious amounts of trash-talking from wrestlers like Bret "The Hitman" Hart, Randy "Macho Man" Savage and Rowdy Roddy Piper. After a terrible struggle, I finally got Super Sam into my submission hold — the one that nobody had ever escaped from.

From somewhere deep inside, Super Sam began drawing on hidden resources of energy. A flailing hand caught me on the side of the head and sent me reeling across the room. In my daze, I lost track of my would-be assailant. Super Sam, sensing my confusion, climbed onto the top rope (the night table). With a mighty flying leap, he delivered the paralyzing, double-kneed back drop. This sent me into convulsions, flopping and spazzing about. As my over-embellished contortions slowed (I hovered between unconsciousness and a coma), Super Sam pinned my shoulders: "One! two!"

My left shoulder popped up. Super Sam pinned me down again: "One! two!"

I lifted my right shoulder. Realizing there was still some fight left in his mortal enemy, Super Sam administered a back-hand karate chop to my adams apple, following up with a two-hand choke hold. I struggled to break his grip, double-chopped his neck, gave him a thumb to the eye — but nothing fazed him. My arms flopped down, my head lolled to one side, my tongue hung out. Super Sam pinned my shoulders one last time: "One! two! three! You're dead, sucker! Super Sam rules!"

Around the room he strutted (Mohammed-Ali

style) as I slowly came to and immediately began protesting the match — though to no avail.

After a healthy, nutricious meal of grilled cheese sandwiches, french fries and ketchup, off we went to the indoor pool. We found it empty and the game of choice turned to football. Sam would run towards the pool and I would throw the nerf football so he could leap, make a mid-air grab and then splash down into the pool. The quarterback's "pocket" was a hot tub situated immediately beside the pool. This allowed me to stay warm, cozy and protected from defensive linemen. Sam would climb out of the water and take up his ready position. I'd cry: "Blue 23, Blue 23, Hike!" Sam would run his pattern and I would arc the ball to him. He made some nice grabs but after half an hour, and once Sam had swallowed his own body weight in water, we headed for the shower.

To our dismay, we discovered only one towel. To determine who would wear it back to the room, I proposed that we do rock, paper, scissors. I knew Sam always picked paper, so to secure the towel and maintain my modesty, I picked scissors. After our shower, I let Sam towel off first, but when he was done, he faced a dilemma — whether to put on a cold wet bathing suit or run bare naked back to the room. Being a five-year-old, Sam created a third option. He took a paper towel to cover his "front privates" and used his free hand to cover "rear privates." Ready to leave, he made the mistake of asking if I could see anything. "Oh, my gosh, Sam — I can see almost all your butt crack."

Deeply concerned, Sam decided to use another paper towel to cover the southern exposure.

Entering the elevator produced another challenge. Sam loved to push the buttons but to do that, he would have to give up vital cover. On his terse instructions, I checked both ways and announced: "The coast is clear." Sam sacrificed his southern exposure and pushed the right button. Reaching our floor, Sam squealed with delight as he raced ahead of me down the hall to our room. The paper towels flapped and his legs flailed (exposing all) as he squealed with delight, flip-flopping down the hall. I busted a gut, witnessing my boy at his very best.

That afternoon at the All-Star Game, I watched the finest hockey players in the world go at it for sixty minutes. Eight NHL mascots had turned up and Sam spent most of his time playing with them while eating popcorn and drinking coke. He would hug and high-five each mascot and take a candy or two from each before seeing the rest flung into the audience. He then enjoyed the antics of each mascot, rather than the game, from the best seat in the house — my lap.

Returning home, Sam laid his head on my knee as the airplane taxied down the runway and didn't move a muscle until we touched down in Calgary. As we walked in the door, Dawn asked if we had enjoyed the game. "Sure we did," I responded. "But the pre-game show at the hotel was way better!"

CHAPTER ELEVEN

TEARS IN HEAVEN

Because most of Sam's young friends would be present, we felt it would be inappropriate to have a funeral with a body, a casket or even ashes. We thought we should have a memorial, a living tribute to Sam. A good friend of ours, Jode Weinberger (Dwight's wife), took charge. She began gathering Sam's favourite things — hockey sweaters, pictures poems, artwork, toys.

Dawn and I agreed to hold the service at the Millarville elementary school gymnasium. The local pastor, Richard Erb, had helped us decide what what was appropriate and what was inappropriate. Slowly, the pieces started to fit together. The memorial service for our son Samuel Jess Johnson was scheduled for Saturday, April 10, 1999, at eleven o'clock in the morning.

The night before, as usual now, I slept fitfully or not at all. In the morning I awoke from a nightmare only to realize that the nightmare I was living was far worse. From the time we had received the phone call in Banff until now seemed to be seamless, almost a single moment in time. I felt like a cork bobbing in a tumultuous, gale-tossed ocean.

We gathered at the kitchen table and ate breakfast in silence, separately and sporadically. I read the eulogy one final time and made a photocopy, thinking that if I proved unable to deliver the message, perhaps I would ask our close friend Don Campbell or the pastor to do so. Snow had fallen during the night, covering the rolling hills with a brilliant white blanket. We quietly donned our Sunday-best clothes, left the house and climbed into the family vehicle. At the highway we came to a full stop and waited while three different vehicles drove past with people we recognized — all of us going to the same place. The neighbor's snow-bright fields made me wonder: this was not a day for a memorial service, but rather a day to go tobogganning down those shining hills, to go running and laughing and playing.

Sam had started playschool in Millarville two years before, in the fall of 1997. The arrangement was that the kindergarten kids went to school in the morning and the same teacher, Mrs. Draper, worked with the playschool kids in the afternoon. Each morning we would roust the children from their warm and comfy beds at seven a.m. and make them breakfast. Then either Dawn or I would walk Patches (the family dog) and the three girls down our long, fairly steep hill to the blue teepee at the front entrance of our property and wait for the yellow and black school bus.

The walk was half a kilometer long and the return hike presented a reasonable challenge. The round trip was invigorating and the company always good. With Sam in playschool and not due at school until the afternoon, Dawn and I allowed him to sleep in. He had no trouble dozing through the commotion of his three sisters brushing their teeth, putting on their clothes, making their beds, and clamoring to get out the door on time. His own mornings were long and lazy.

Around ten or eleven, he would moan and stretch and then sleepily make his way to the bathroom and then to the kitchen counter. There, clad only in his

Superman underwear and with a blanket over his shoulders, he would enjoy his breakfast and conversation. Often I would tease him: "It's great work . . . if you can find it!"

Starting in September of 1998, Sam faced a dramatically different routine. The little guy now had to rise and shine at 0700 hours, just like his sisters, and trot down the drive to catch the bus. This arrangement never really appealed to him. He would rise, all right, but he wouldn't shine — not until much later in the day.

When Sam began attending school in the morning, I set up my work days so I could work when he was absent, making most of my telephone calls between eight and quarter past eleven. This freed the afternoons for Sam and, when the girls arrived, the whole family. Promptly at eleven fifteen, Monday through Thursday, Dawn or I or the two of us would drive the six miles into Millarville to pick up Sam from kindergarten. For me, this simple act proved a special joy.

After dismissal, Sam would run over, take me by the hand and guide me enthusiastically over to view his latest artistic accomplishment — a painting, a drawing or a craft he had completed that day. My all-time favorite was a painting he had done depicting himself on a blue motorcycle, waving. Beneath it he had written, "Thanks for the birthday present, Dad."

Every time I look at that painting, I remember Sam's dogged quest for a motorcycle and how that played out. The essence of Sam, the boy's very soul, had ached for a blue motorcycle. Whenever he and I would go for a drive, Sam would gaze out the window. More than once, I asked him, "What you thinkin' 'bout, little buddy?"

Without deliberation, he would answer: "A motorcycle, Dad."

"What kind of motorcycle, Sam?" As if I needed to ask.

His voice would build with enthusiasm as he responded: "A blue, very fast, very COOL motorcycle."

You could wake Sam at 3 a.m. from a dead sleep, ask him what he was thinking and he would respond in the same way. He lobbied like this for more than a year. One night, when all the kids were in bed and fast asleep, and with his sixth birthday just around the corner (March 15), I took Sam's case to the highest court in the land. The more Dawn and I discussed it, the more clearly we realized that a $1,500 mini-bike was simply too extravagant a gift for any one of our children. Then Dawn (brilliant as always) suggested, "What if we give the motorcycle to the whole family before his birthday, and then give Sam blue motorcycle-riding gloves on his actual birthday?"

The idea was sound. Giving the bike to the family would elminate the possessive mentality: "Don't touch it, it's mine." It would also preclude requests like, "Sam got a motorcycle for his birthday, I want…."

The following Friday, to add some considerable fun to the experience, Sam and I drove to the city to window shop. I decided to go to Blackfoot Motorcycles, the largest motorcycle showroom in Calgary — but I didn't tell Sam. As we approached the store, I told Sam to close his eyes and no peeking allowed. On arriving in the parking lot, I insisted that he keep his eyes closed, so adding to his anticipation. I went round to his side of the vehicle, opened the door and guided him, with his eyes still closed, all the way across the lot and through the front door of the showroom. Then, after counting down from ten to one ("five, four, three. . ."), I told him, "Surprise! Open your eyes!"

Sam opened his eyes and discovered himself surrounded by no fewer than one hundred brand-spanking-new, brightly polished, beautifully lit machines — everything from motorcycles, sea-doos and quads to scooters and mini-bikes — together with matching paraphernalia.

Sam cried, "Wow, Dad!" with all the wonder and enthusiasm of a five-year-old.

For the next few minutes, we roamed among sea-doos, quads and large touring bikes, and finally we reached the mini-bikes. Once in this section, I relaxed and simply enjoyed my boy totally enjoying himself. With little to-do, Sam picked out a blue (very cool) Yamaha PW-50 mini-bike. He played on it until well after I had made the deal on its twin and had it loaded into the back of the Suburban under a blanket I had brought for exactly this purpose.

All the way home, Sam enthusiastically inquired, "When can we go back there again?"

That Saturday morning, two days before Sam's birthday, and after the kids had watered and picked up after the dog and cats, Dawn and I assembled the gang on the porch. There sat a surprise, carefully hidden under a blanket. Each of the kids took hold of the blanket, and on the count of three, pulled it off to reveal . . . the family mini-bike!

Levi was too young fully to understand, but Juli, Laura and Alana gushed excitedly, while Sam went beyond gushing. For once in his young life, he was speechless. The four eldest played Rock, Paper, Scissors to see who would get the first ride, and sure enough, Sam got the maiden voyage.

I had chosen a mini-bike with an adjustable set screw that enabled me to control the amount of throttle to be used. After giving a lesson on usage and adjusting the screw to its safest setting, I watched all morning and most of the afternoon as an endless rotation of Johnsons explored every square foot of our homestead on the blue mini-bike.

Dawn later summed it up best: "For them, it's a taste of freedom."

93

By the end of the first week, the kids knew the drill: come home from school, look after the dog and cats, check the mini-bike for oil and gas, Rock/Paper/Scissors to see who would go in what order and then start the rotation, ten minutes each at a time. As the oldest, Juli used her watch to time each rider, and for the most part was scrupulously fair.

Once all four older children were riding confidently, I backed off the set screw to allow them to set their own pace. There were a few garden variety spills but the single spectacular crash was left to the kid who knew no human boundaries . . . Super Sam Johnson.

As a general rule, and with their confidence growing, the non-riding children would play on the trampoline while waiting their turn to zoom around on the mini-bike. This particular evening, I happened to be working on the porch. I glanced up just as Sam, roaring along at full speed, rode the mini-bike straight into the trampoline. He struck the edge with the middle of his chest and instantly stopped in mid-air, leaving the bike to continue down the road without a rider.

Dawn was at his side in a heartbeat and I arrived a second later. She established that Sam was breathing but feared he was seriously hurt: how could he not be? We did not want to move him but Sam started moaning and whimpering and insisted on getting to his feet. Together, we made our way to the cottage.

There, after we'd determined that Sam had only had the wind knocked out of him, Sam filled us in on the rest of the story. He was riding the bike under full throttle and hit a patch of loose gravel that turned him directly towards "the tramp." He couldn't react quickly enough to avoid the collision.

After hearing this, I called all the children together and issued some additional rules about using half throttle anywhere near the house and full throttle only down in the pasture. As for Sam, he dusted himself off and rejoined the rotation. No way he was going to miss an evening on the mini-bike.

That was Sam. No matter what he did, he was "hell bent for election." When he got knocked down, he would get right back up again. If he got thrown off, he would climb right back into the saddle. Sam feared nothing. Often, his lack of fear amazed me.

My afternoons with Sam were among the highlights of any week. Sam was an afternoon person. He sparkled from noon on. After viewing what he had accomplished at kindergarten, usually we would visit the Millarville General Store, where I would collect the mail and a newspaper, and then we would head home for lunch.

In Millarville, kindergarten runs Monday to Thursday. Sam had no commitments for Friday, which by coincidence was often a *free day* for me. Friday mornings, I would get everybody up at seven o'clock, including Sam. We would see the girls off to school and then Sam and I would head into town to do all of the family chores — drop off the dry cleaning, pick up some groceries, rent a good movie, whatever.

On Fridays, we also tried to work special events into our schedule. When the International Car Show came to Calgary, Sam and I arrived promptly at ten o'clock just as the doors opened. We bought our tickets and walked hand in hand straight to Tiny Tim's donut kiosk. Both Sam and I were big fans of these tiny donuts sprinkled liberally with sugar and cinnamon. I would squeeze a dollar into his hand so he could buy his own, and then the two of us would hustle, Three Stooges-style, to see who could get into line first.

I have long been interested in the technology of the automobile and enjoyed the chance to see the latest changes and all the different vehicles under one roof. Sam's priorities were different. He gravitated towards the concept cars, any vehicles painted blue (by far his favorite color), and of course any thing he thought was "way cool." We strolled around and then Sam would see a vehicle that he wanted to get into. We would dust the cinnamon sugar off his hands, I would open the door like a chauffeur and say, "Your vehicle is ready, Master Johnson." He would climb in behind the wheel, pretend to start up the car and provide his own sound effects for the motor, squealing tires and hard breaking.

After we had browsed for a couple of hours and run out of money for donuts, we headed for the door. We made one or two quick stops as we left town, and about five minutes out onto Highway 22X, Sam drifted off to sleep. Reaching over with one hand, I reclined his seat a bit farther so that he would be more comfortable and threw my jacket over him. For the next thirty minutes, as my son slept beside me, I basked in the glory of the relationship that he and I shared.

Now, arrived at the school for the memorial service, as Dawn and I and the girls exited our vehicle and started towards the "teachers only" doors — reserved that particular day for our grieving family — we noticed that some kind souls had tied dozens of bright yellow ribbons around two trees, creating a vivid image against the backdrop of new snow. I remember Dawn stopping to admire this handiwork almost in disbelief. We were truly touched by the gesture.

After our extended families had gathered in a classroom, the pastor arrived and said, "It's time." Dawn and I led the procession, holding the hands of our children, and sat down in the front row of the gymnasium. Immediately before me was the podium. Some thoughtful person had blown up an eight-by-

Sam and me at the end of
a full day.

Mom and Sam making do
at the cottage.

Sam and his best buddy, Ester.

At Disney World,
Sam simply ran
out of gas.

One of my all time
favorite group shots.

Sam 's favorite
red fire truck.

Celebrating Christmas at a friend's home.

Alana, Juli,
Frosty and Sam.

Sam's first day
at pre-school,
Sept. 1/97.

Sam and Alana
at Lake Louise.

Halloween '97:
Sam as Woody and Dad
as a Hanson Brother.

When he was beat, he was beat.

Cousins and
siblings at
the lake.

Cheeseburger
in paradise.

Sam being Sam.

The "Goof Troop" with their fearless leader.

Our whole crew played STARS basketball.

Repeating our vows on our 10th anniversary with Sam as best man.

The boy loved his hockey.

Sam's last Christmas: no doubt asking for a blue motorcycle.

Sam and Laura admiring their one-minute-old brother, Levi.

Our last family photo: October'98.

The day after the tragedy

Sam's kindergarten
picture, '98.

ten picture of Sam, framed it, and placed it underneath the podium.

The service opened not with a traditional hymn, but rather with John Lennon's Beautiful Boy. Then, after reading most of Psalm 139 ("Lord, thou hast searched me, and known me"), and saying a prayer, pastor Richard Erb offered a meditation, based on the Book of John, in which he observed that the miracle of the loaves and fishes began when "a small boy, whose name we do not know, came forward with five small barley loaves and two small fish."

The pastor continued: "Sam brought much to the people around him. His energy and his enthusiasm for life was contagious to the people around him. Our tendency in this tragic situation is to look at Sam's life like the few small barley loaves and two small fish. To say: 'There needs to be much more....There should have been much more....So much that could have been.'

"John's gospel tells us that when everybody had eaten, Jesus said: 'Don't waste anything.' And they gathered up twelve basketfuls of leftovers. One for each of the twelve disciples who had seen the boy come forward. I believe that today, and the days ahead, should be a time for gathering up basketfuls. To think of the many ways that Sam in his enthusiasm touched the people around him, and to gather up and cherish all we have from Sam's life."

The pastor's meditation was very moving. Four or five young people from the church provided musical accompaniment. The principal of the school, Tony Hampshire, talked about the shock and the tragedy of losing someone at such a young age. I was drifting mentally when the pastor came over and said, "It's your turn."

I stood up, unfolded my notes and, for the first time, looked up and realized that the gymnasium was beyond full — it was jam-packed. Every seat was taken, all standing room was occupied, and people were spilling out into the hallway. I later learned that the seating capacity of the gymnasium is two hundred, though with standing room it holds two hundred and forty. On this Saturday, however, more than three hundred and fifty people had crowded into the gymnasium, while another one hundred and fifty had gathered in the hallway and the library, where stereo speakers piped in the service.

I found it extremely difficult to start the eulogy. I was crying so hard that I couldn't read my notes. Yet I didn't want anyone else to deliver the message: this was my job. I drew on something deep down inside and managed to begin:

> On behalf of Sam and our family, I would like to thank all of you for your support at this difficult time. Samuel Jess Johnson was six years old when he suddenly passed away April 8, 1999. He is survived by myself, his mother Dawn, his sisters Juli (age ten), Laura (eight), Alana (seven), and his younger brother, Levi (one and a half).
>
> Sam was a young man with boundless energy, a true zest for life, and a wonderful, infectious, radiant smile. He had a marvelous passion for all sports: hockey, baseball, soccer, basketball and, especially, our version of WWF Wrestling, which our family calls "King or Queen of the Bed!"
>
> Sam lived a great deal of his life vicariously through characters like Buz Light-year, Woody, Superman, Spiderman and Batman and his own WWF creation. This last character sported a cape, make-up and a pair of shorts pulled high above his navel. He was "Super Sam." When Sam put on his "Super Sam" costume, he was instantly transformed into a trash-talking King of the Bed

competitor, and was famous internationally for three patented wrestling moves: Karate chop to the throat; the errant elbow or knee to the groin; and the flying double-knee back-drop off the dresser. (This move was performed when the victim was incapacitated or looking the other way.)

Many of the characteristics that his heroes and super-heroes possessed, like dashing good looks, super-human strength, x-ray vision, courage, valor, honesty and fear-lessness, were shared by Sam himself. Numerous times he was rescued from dangerous situations as he simply refused to heed warnings, discipline, and punishment for venturing into perilous situations that would challenge even the most powerful super hero.

And so it was on Wednesday April 7, 1999, that Sam, after repeated warnings, followed his dog Patches out onto the thin ice of our pond in Millarville, probably to look for tennis balls, hockey pucks or geese nests. In any event, it was this adventurous nature of his that led to his early departure from us.

Naturally we are sad and hurt and miss Sam terribly. However, we are at peace in knowing that we loved and adored him to such a great degree. We know in our hearts that he lived a full and extremely happy life. Once again, thank you to all who loved Sam.

The song we chose to end the service was Eric Clapton's *Tears in Heaven*.

The pastor thanked people for coming and announced that there would be a reception in the library. Our family was ushered out. We retreated into a nearby room, where in privacy, Dawn and I composed ourselves. After a few minutes, we re-emerged and stood beside the memorial table that had been erected for Sam, Dawn on one side, myself on the other.

For the next hour and a half, I hugged everyone who approached. I heard people say over and over and over again how sorry they were, how much they cared for Sam, and was there anything they could do. After what seemed an endless sea of people, the procession mercifully came to an end. I was totally drained, not only emotionally but physically as well. I had psyched myself up for an extremely difficult event, and now that it was over, I just wanted to go home with my family.

Back at the house, I traded my suit and tie for a comfortable track suit. I began to relax. I felt a sense of relief: we had completed a big job. My closest friends and family were now around me and for the first time in four days, I felt able to enter into a conversation about something other than the loss of my son.

I'm not sure how it began, but we all found ourselves looking through the many photo albums Dawn and I had compiled over the years. People opened them and left them in different parts of the house — a couple on the dining room table, one on the kitchen countertop, another by the fireplace. We flipped through the pages looking at our children from when they were born, through their first pairs of shoes, on to their first tricycles, then their bicycles, the school plays, the picnics, the summer holidays, all of it captured by the camera and stored chronologically. Everybody seemed to enjoy looking through these albums as much as we did, seeing our family growing through happier times — above all, seeing Sam in different situations. It had a therapeutic affect.

Around seven o'clock that night, well-wishers

started to excuse themselves, saying things like, "We'll leave this with you, let us know if we can do anything, we'll drop in tomorrow." On the latter topic, as politely as we could, we told people, "Thank you very much, but we don't want people dropping in. We know that we have some serious work to do, and we really feel a need for privacy."

That night, after the kids had gone to bed, Dawn and I put our house back together again, returning items to the fridge and loading the dishwasher. It was about then I started to feel desperate. I started to feel anguish, deep anguish. I started to feel emotions I had never felt before.

The momentary relief I had felt after returning from the service had vanished. I now felt myself tumbling into a vast chasm of grief, sighting depths that I had not yet explored. My head ached and pounded. I felt desperately sad. My lungs felt crushed, my ribs like they were broken. I couldn't get enough air. I went for a short walk but it didn't help. I didn't know what kind of a problem I was having, but I knew I was having some sort of breakdown.

Frantically, I phoned the local doctor who had delivered our youngest son, Levi. I told him, through tears and in jerky sentences, that I was falling apart. To his credit, he never once said to me, "Hey, listen, Tim, I know what you're going through." He simply broke into what must have been a mental checklist. He asked questions like: are you getting any sleep? have you been eating? have you been drinking fluids? have you been drinking alcohol?

As he ran down the checklist, I found myself getting answers. I told him that I hadn't slept much, if at all, since Tuesday night. That I wasn't eating much and wasn't drinking any alcohol. He said that what was going on with me was quite normal. He hesitated to give me anything for the pain, or

101

anything to help me sleep, but explained that my body had just gone through a very traumatic experience. I was reacting to it. He said that the best thing I could do is relax, take some deep breaths, take an aspirin if I had to, but get some sleep. I felt somewhat comforted by what he said. I took an aspirin and went out to the Quonset hut where I could sleep alone.

After an hour or more of fidgeting and twitching, tossing and turning, finally I drifted off.

CHAPTER TWELVE

EASTER HOLIDAYS

Mornings have always been my best time. To get up early, enjoy the sunrise, savor a part of the day that most people never see — this is an experience I enjoy very much. That Sunday morning after the memorial service, I got up early and went for a short walk. On returning to the house, I felt not too bad.

By contrast, Dawn had entered what I would call "full grieving mode." She was weeping, incoherent, and didn't know even that I was in the same room. For some reason, with her in such despair, I found it impossible to do any grieving myself. I found comfort in tending to the house, the needs and wants of the kids, and in allowing Dawn to do what she had to do.

The phone calls had tapered off. A few supporting families came and went with food, flowers and cards. In mid-afternoon, my three girls announced that they wanted a driving lesson in our beat-up work truck. I jumped at the opportunity. Relief at last. I instructed them one by one to apply a little more gas with the right foot while working the clutch pedal with the left. As we jerked and lurched around the property, I found myself enjoying my children as they turned our old white pick-up truck into a reasonable facsimile of the Indiana Jones Ride at Disney World. This session in the truck reminded me of how, a few months previous, I'd suggested to Dawn that we might take Easter break in the month of March and head off to Orlando, Florida and Disney World for nine days. This would include the week that the kids would be out of school as well as the weekend before their Easter vacation. We had been living in confined quarters for eighteen months and the dark days of winter were setting in. I felt it would be nice to stay at the Disney resort and enjoy a really good holiday in a warm climate.

We talked this over for a while but eventually agreed that it would not work. Levi, our youngest, was now eighteen months and walking, talking and getting into everything. He was the centre of the universe and knew it — a non-stop, Tasmanian devil from the moment he awoke until at the end of the day he would finally just flop over somewhere and fall asleep. Levi was extremely demanding, a really busy young fellow. As much as Dawn and I searched our minds, we could not remember any of the other four kids being nearly that busy.

Levi was not ready to be entertained by Mickey, Goofy or any of the rides at Disney World. He would demand our undivided attention. We considered perhaps leaving him behind with a caregiver and just going down with the four older children, but the more we talked about that, the more we felt that it just wouldn't be a family vacation without Levi. Ultimately, we decided we wouldn't do it this year but next, during the winter of 2000, when Levi would be one year more mature.

As with Christmas, then, we decided to spend Easter of 1999 hanging out as a family in Millarville. We had great fun coloring Easter eggs around the dinner table — giggling, kibitzing and then proudly displaying our artistic talents. On Easter Sunday, we hid Easter eggs, opened presents and ate chocolate bunnies instead of eggs and toast. I remember distinctly the love that Dawn had put into buying gifts, wrapping them and hiding them in all the nooks and crannies of the cabin. Dawn, far better than me, knew how to celebrate holidays, how to turn them into events.

She would immerse herself in the tradition of each holiday, decorating, creating crafts or doing something special with the kids. This was so different from the holidays I experienced as a boy, when any holiday, even Christmas, became a hassle. My mother did all the work. My father believed that the woman was supposed to buy the gifts, pick out the tree and decorate the house, in addition to handling the additional seasonal cooking and cleaning. He also had an inability to relax or be still: if he wasn't working, he was drinking. Holidays were tough on him and consequently on all of us.

This background meant that as an adult, even when I wanted to join in on the holiday festivities, often I didn't know how. Dawn was very good about suggesting, or leading, or getting me involved. At Christmas she would say, "You know, if you go get three strings of lights and the staple gun, you could put up the decorations around the house." I had never seen this done, and I never really expected that I would do this, but the more that I participated in the holiday, the more I would enjoy it.

Easter was very much like that. I enjoyed the hiding and hunting of eggs, the stuffing of faces with chocolate. The whole season appealed — days of getting up early and clomping around in our pajamas until the early afternoon, goofing off and not eating from the suggested food groups. In any event, this particular Easter holiday brought about all kinds of warm and fuzzy feelings.

The Wednesday after Easter Sunday, Dawn and I planned to leave the kids in Millarville with a caregiver and spend a couple of days and nights in

Banff, where I had a business workshop to attend. So, on the day before we were due to leave, the Tuesday, I loaded the four oldest kids into the Suburban and drove into Calgary. We ate breakfast at McDonald's and then headed for our all-time favorite toy store. Before leaving the vehicle, we all had to agree: "We can look but we are not buying anything today, right?" The children moaned but I reminded them that, if they were good, maybe tomorrow the caregiver would bring them back. They accepted that and tumbled out of the car and raced to the front door.

Once inside, the kids scattered, seeking out a Gameboy or a Sony Play Station demonstration where they could actually demo a couple of games. The store had a bicycle in one of the aisles and a couple of the kids took turns riding it. The girls enjoyed looking over the Barbie collection, examining things they would like to own and dreaming of the type of Barbie they would like next Christmas — even if it was nine months away.

Sam was drawn to the superheroes section, which featured Batman, Spiderman, Superman, Robin and all the other action figures and really "cool" accessories. He reveled in this environment. As for me, I took what was left of my coffee and walked casually up and down the aisles looking at the games, puzzles and toys. As often before, we spent an hour or more just hanging out in the store.

On that particular Tuesday, April 6, 1999, after eating breakfast and visiting the toy store, we decided to find a matinee showing of a movie called *The King of Egypt*. Instead of picking up a newspaper, we drove to one mall, then another, and another, but we could not find a matinee. We ended up visiting four different movie theatres before finally we learned that matinees did not happen on Tuesdays, not even during the Easter holiday, and would only be run on the weekend.

After phoning Dawn from the car and telling her about the matinee problem, we started wending our way home. Dawn had requested some groceries and we stopped at Superstore to get them. Sam was riding in the shopping cart, with Laura pushing it and Alana riding on the outside, when Juli showed up drinking a nice cold Coke. Oh, oh, I thought. This is going to be trouble.

All our kids receive a monthly allowance. The younger ones, Sam and Alana, tended to blow the money quickly, but the older ones, Juli and Laura, would hang onto it more. The "Johnson Rule" is that, if you have your own money, you can spend it, but no begging Mom or Dad for stuff if you don't. So, although Juli was technically playing by the rules, I knew this was going to create havoc. Seeing her Coke, Laura and Alana simultaneously spouted, "Can I have a drink?" Before Juli could say no, I jumped in (knowing this thing could blow up real fast): "Juli, I know you bought that with your own money, but Mom will have supper waiting for us, and you know that if you had asked my permission, I would have said no. Now, please give everyone a drink (as penance) and then finish the Coke by the door so the other kids don't have to watch you."

Alana took a sip and then Laura gulped down a couple of healthy swallows before Juli grabbed the can out of her hands, splashing Laura's hands and the floor beside the cart with sticky brown cola. Juli cried: "Laura, that's not fair and you know it!"

"Give me the Coke," I said. "What's up with you guys?"

I was irritated both at Juli's poor judgement and Laura's lack of respect. Turning to Sam I said, "Take your drink." With his arms folded and his head down in defiance, he said, "I want my own Coke."

My temperature rising, I said: "Fine — then you'll have none."

I handed Juli her Coke: "Go wait at the front of the store with this."

While the rest of us joined the checkout line, Juli continued to enjoy her drink in full view of her "parched" siblings. As I lifted Sam out of the cart, he went from sulking to throwing a full-fledged temper tantrum. As we began leaving the building, he flopped into the corner underneath the softdrink machine in the breezeway and declared: "I'm staying right here until you buy me a Coke."

Dawn and I share a common view. We don't give in just because one of our children decides to throw a fit, even to kick and scream and holler. As long as the child is in a safe environment, we let the tantrum run its course. We all waited while Sam carried on. The girls had some coloring and reading to do in the Suburban, so I decided to walk outside, load up all the kids (except Sam), start the truck, drive around in a semi-circle and park near the front doors so I could watch and wait until Sam decided to finish.

Once we were all strapped in, I pulled out to make my turn. Sam came screaming out the front doors: "Stop! Stop, don't leave me!" I stopped in the middle of the lane, jumped out and scooped him up in both arms. Hysterically, he continued to protest: "Don't leave me! Don't leave me!"

"Sam, Sam, settle down," I said. "Settle down and understand something. I will never, ever, ever leave you, ever. Do you understand?"

Eventually, he replied through sobs and tears: "Yes, but I thought you were going to leave me."

"Sam, I will never leave you," I said. Then I repeated something we had told our children many, many times: "If you ever do get lost, we will never stop looking for you. We will keep looking for you until we find you."

In retrospect, those words carry a special meaning for me. Since Sam passed, people have often said,

"We are sorry you lost your son." And I always want to answer, "I didn't lose Sam. He still exists...just in another realm."

At the time, Sam seemed to be considerably eased by what I said, and after he calmed down, I belted him into his seat, mussed his hair and set out for Millarville. We still had a few chores to do, among them renting a movie. The only one we could all agree on was *Vampires*, a John Carpenter film starring James Wood and one of the Baldwin brothers, so we rented that.

Back home, we ate a fine dinner that Dawn had prepared and then, while we adults cleaned up, the kids played together. As the evening wore on, Dawn suggested that the kids should brush their teeth and go straight to bed. Wanting especially to make it up with Sam, I pleaded their case: "Dawn, they're on holiday. We've picked out a movie. You and I are going to be away for a few days. Maybe it would be a good idea for all of us to watch the movie together."

Dawn conceded but still had packing to do and so declined to join us. The children and I retreated down the hill to the rustic Quonset hut, which housed my office but doubled as a TV movie-viewing room. As it was a bit cool, I built a small fire in the potbelly stove and sat down to enjoy the movie with the kids. I have a favorite black leather chair, and I reclined it slightly and invited Sam to sit on my knee. He surprised me by sitting still and not shifting around. I ended up spending the whole evening with him sitting in my lap, his right hand holding my thumb. When I was a boy about Sam's age, I chronically chewed my right thumb nail and, as a result, it grows oddly. Sam ran his index finger up, down and all around, exploring the odd shape of it.

When the last vampire lay slain and the sun rose on the little Texas town that had now been exorcised by James Wood and his vampire slayers, I announced,

"Bed time!" The Quonset hut lies about one hundred feet south of the house. As usual, I proposed to give the kids a twenty-foot head start and then to give chase. If I caught them before they reached the front door of the cabin, I got to spank them on the bum. I cried, "Go!" And four squealing kids took off across the lawn towards the house. I managed to overtake them and give a couple a swat, but realized that soon, I might have to cut their lead in half.

In the house, as the kids took turns brushing their teeth, a wrestling match erupted. One of the kids tackled me onto the king-sized bed in our bedroom and the three other children jumped in immediately. I've often noticed that, if my children enjoy a movie, they immediately become the characters in that movie. For example, when Sam watched *Toy Story*, he became Woody, and he remained Woody for the next six to eight weeks. Alana, after she watched *Aladdin*, became Jasmine for the longest time.

Now, having watched a knock 'em down, drag 'em out, vampire-slaying movie, the kids cast me in the role of the unbitten victim, while they themselves became four thirsty, blood-sucking vampires. Soon I was fighting for my mortal life. I was doing my best to ward off the vampires, but they ignored all the usual remedies. I held my fingers in a cross, I managed to turn on the lights in the bedroom, I even told them I'd had garlic for supper — nothing phased them.

At one point, the three girls got me into an awkward position and Sam, sensing my weariness, took full advantage. He put his knees on my chest, pulled my hair until I exposed my neck and he could get down to bite me "vampire fashion." The whole evening had been so much fun that I found myself laughing uncontrollably. The harder I laughed, the more the kids enjoyed it and the less capable I became of defending myself.

Because of the beating and biting I was enduring, I realized that, next morning, I would almost certainly turn into a vampire. At last Dawn rescued me by coming into the bedroom and announcing that enough was enough: Levi was sleeping in the next room and we should be respectful of him. It was time for good little kids and vampires alike to go to bed. We coaxed them into their respective beds. Juli slept on the top bunk, Laura and Alana shared the bottom, double-bunk, and from beneath that bunk, for Sam, we pulled out the foam mattress and placed it up against the wall. Now we had a heart-to-heart talk. This was a chance for everyone just before bed to vent, telling what they liked or didn't like about the day. We went around the circle asking who wanted to share first.

Juli talked about how much fun it was wrestling and being a vampire. Laura said she had seen a horse at the toy store that she wanted to buy it with her next allowance. Alana talked about something so obscure that nobody could understand where she had spent the day (although she had spent it with us). Sam said he didn't like it when he thought we were going to leave him behind at the Superstore. With a devilish grin, he also mentioned that he really liked sucking my blood. Dawn and I added our two cents worth, pecked the kids on their cheeks and told them how much we loved them. As we turned off the lights, Sam said something quite out of character: "Tomorrow morning when you get up, make sure you wake me so I can kiss you goodbye."

"Well, you'll probably be sleeping deeply," Dawn said. "We're leaving pretty early."

Sam said, "No, even if you have to bonk me on the head, you get me up so I can say goodbye to you...promise?"

Dawn and I promised, crossed our hearts and retired early.

CHAPTER THIRTEEN

APRIL 7, 1999

During the months that followed Sam's passing, through conversations with those who were there, mainly the children, I began piecing together the events of the day: April 7, 1999. After Dawn and I had left for Banff, the kids rolled out of bed and ate a leisurely breakfast. They spent a lazy Saturday morning playing together. After lunch, the caregiver, "Barbara," piled the children into our suburban and drove into Calgary — back to our favorite toy store. The night before, we had given them their allowance, and now, as arranged, they could enjoy it.

Arriving back at the Millarville homestead, Barbara was pleased and surprised to find that her husband, "Robert," had arrived with hamburgers and plans for a barbecue. The day was sunny and warm. Robert fired up the on-deck barbecue and the children played with their new toys. Barbara had purchased a multi-colored beach ball for eighteen-month-old Levi. Sam took a liking to it and began kicking it around, monopolizing it. Barbara took the ball away from him, returned it to Levi and told Sam to play with his own new blue ray gun.

Once Levi had abandoned the ball for another toy, Sam asked Barbara if he could take the beach ball outside to play with it. She gave him permission. Shortly thereafter, Sam returned to the cottage to confess that he had accidentally punctured the ball. Barbara scolded him in front of his three sisters and Robert.

Dawn and I had told Barbara that the children were not to leave the house unaccompanied, partly on principle, partly because bears and cougars have been known to turn up in the vicinity. But Barbara must have wanted Sam really to think about what he had done and how he could make amends. She told him to walk down the gravel drive to the blue teepee — and then to walk back. Upon his return, they would have a little chat.

As a father, several things strike me as odd about this development. Sam had permission to play with the ball and accidentally popped it. He confessed immediately. Barbara seemed to over-react: sending Sam to the teepee meant a half-kilometer trip in each direction. The punishment didn't fit the crime. It was "way harsh." Sam was perhaps a bit careless or out of bounds in his use of his brother's new toy, but Barbara was way out of bounds in sending one of the children, unaccompanied, anywhere on the property. Further, Sam probably felt embarrassed, hurt and victimized. He might have left right away, but certainly he would not have been in any hurry to return.

Sam took his friend Patches, our border collie, and headed down the hill. Barbara went back into the house. Robert, who earns his living as a paramedic, remained on the deck with the girls and started the barbecue. After fifteen or twenty minutes, Barbara emerged from the house: "Has anyone seen Sam?"

Nobody had seen the little guy. After some discussion with Robert, Barbara jumped into her half-ton truck and drove down the hill to the teepee. No sign of Sam.

Barbara returned to the house and asked

everyone if they had seen him. No's all around. Taking Juli Ann, at age ten the oldest of the girls, Barbara drove back down to the teepee. She would have glanced over at the pond, clearly visible behind a barbed-wire fence about a hundred yards to her left, and must have thought, no way: the pond is strictly off-limits. She knew I had repeatedly warned all the children to stay away from the pond: Sam would never go there.

Increasingly worried, verging on panic — where was Sam? — Barbara asked Juli to look inside the blue teepee: no sign of Sam. With Juli, Barbara travelled two miles east and one mile south to check with a neighbour...who hadn't seen our son either. Barbara then drove five miles west along the highway to a another neighbour's house. No, Gail had seen no sign of Sam.

Terrified now, Barbara sped back to our homestead, entering our property at the cattle gate with the blue teepee on her right. Instead of returning to the house, she turned down the dirt feeder road that leads to the fenced-in pond and beyond. She drove right past the pond — Sam would never go in there — and kept going towards the back of our property, racing along the rough dirt road.

Later, Dawn and I were able to piece together how events unfolded. We talked with all the rescue workers, neighbours and the children, studied footprints in the snow and discovered clues around the property...a partially read newspaper lying open beside our bed, the barbecue valve open and the tank empty, the ashes of seven incinerated hamburgers on the grill, a pager and various emergency medical supplies lost in the grass near the pond. Together, they told the story.

When Sam had started kindergarten, he loved riding home on the school bus with his three older sisters, but he hated walking the half kilometer up the hill to our home. Acting on Barbara's stern orders, he had obediently walked downhill to the teepee. But then, to postpone the long walk back up — why would he hurry? just to hear a lecture? — Sam wandered down the road towards the pond. The caregivers' dog, "Cody," trotted down the hill and started playing with Patches. One of the two spotted geese on the pond and decided to give chase. Sam would have followed the dogs through the gate.

Probably, Sam had just arrived at the pond when, for the first time, Barbara drove downhill to the teepee. He knew that if she spotted him near the pond, she would be furious — and so, being a kid, Sam ducked down and hid, either amongst some bullrushes or behind our overturned rowboat on the bank. When the truck disappeared back up the hill, Sam stood watching Cody and Patches thundering back and forth on the ice, scattering geese. The ice held the dogs just fine.

From his strategic hiding spot, Sam would have watched Barbara's truck return to the cottage. He might have heard voices in the distance . . . best to stay hidden. As the truck travelled down the hill a second time, approaching the teepee, Sam would have hidden still lower in the grass, his heart racing. Then, as Barbara swung onto the highway and headed east, he would have felt elated: yes! he had outsmarted the babysitter!

Sam would have turned his attention back to the dogs, who after scattering the geese had probably started wrestling. Springing to his feet, he moved to the edge of the ice-covered pond. The rambunctious energy of the dogs, together with the possibility of discovering geese eggs inside the black tire on the floating dock, proved too much for the boy. A slim fifty-pounder, Sam stepped gingerly onto the frozen pond. The ice held him, no problem. Obviously, his Dad had been far too cautious. With the sun on his back, enjoying himself immensely, Sam made his way across the ice to the dock.

Standing on the ice-bound platform, Sam must have been in heaven. He had eluded Barbara not once but twice. He had proved his Dad wrong: the ice was just fine. His friend Patches was romping nearby. He had found the goose nest empty but full of feathers and new grass that the mother had molded into readiness. With the sun beating down, Sam was perhaps more vitally alive in that moment than he had ever been...at least in this lifetime.

Sam was still on the dock when Barbara returned from visiting neighbours. He heard the truck churning towards him. If the caregiver discovered him here on the pond, where his Dad had warned him not to go, he would be in worse trouble than ever. Sam decided to hide again — and quickly. The truck would be passing on the road that ran outside the fence parallel to the east side of the pond, some twenty meters away. Sam must have thought: *The dock will provide cover. I'll hide behind it.*

Sam jumped off the dock on the west side — and crashed through the ice into the freezing cold water. Suddenly, everything changed. Struggling furiously, trying to pull himself back onto the ice, Sam began hollering for help. More than anything, now, he wanted Barbara to notice him — but the dock concealed him perfectly. Battling frantically, Sam tried to pull himself back onto the ice. Every time he got partway up, the ice broke away. Sam tried to grab hold of the bottom of the deck but it was too high, he couldn't reach. No way he could pull himself onto it. The water felt so cold. Sam continued screaming hysterically: "Help! Help!"

Patches and Cody drew near and began frenziedly barking.

From the deck beside the house, Robert had seen Barbara drive past the pond and continue towards the back of our quarter section. Now he heard the dogs barking and decided to investigate. To Laura, he cried, "Keep an eye on the baby!" Then he jumped onto a bike leaning against the deck and, telling himself this couldn't be happening, raced down the road to the pond. From the far side of the dock, where the dogs continued barking, he heard Sam crying, "Help!"

"I'm coming, Sam! I'm coming!"

A stocky, well-built man weighing maybe one hundred and seventy pounds, Robert stepped onto the ice. Quickly and carefully, like the well-trained professional he was, he began making his way towards the dock. About a third of the way there, roughly fifteen feet out, Robert broke through the ice. Suddenly he found himself in the same predicament as Sam, floundering in freezing cold water. He couldn't believe how cold it was. He tried to pull himself back onto the ice but the ice broke away. He tried again with the same results, and then again, and finally he got back to a spot where, as a muscular adult male, he managed to pull himself to safety.

He could still hear Sam hollering for help, but with far less energy: "Hang on, Sam! I'm coming!"

He needed something to support his weight, something to distribute it on the ice — a ladder, perhaps. Or the rowboat! As he raced toward it, Barbara pulled up in the half-ton. She and Juli Ann jumped out and Robert cried: "Sam's fallen into the pond! Call 911!"

Barbara jumped back into the truck and roared up to the house. Juli Ann raced to the side of the pond. Robert cried: "Stay off the ice!"

He grabbed the overturned rowboat, righted it and dragged it onto the ice.

Juli Ann heard Sam crying from the far side of the dock. She couldn't see him but called, "Hang on, Sam! Robert's coming!"

Robert pushed the boat forward across the ice, hanging onto the back. He managed to get out slightly farther than before but then again the ice gave way. Again Robert found himself floundering in the freezing cold water, breaking ice as he struggled to pull himself into the boat. As a rescue worker, Robert had been well informed and trained in rescue operations involving ice, water and hypothermia. Immersed in water this cold, zero degrees Celsius or colder, people usually lose consciousness within two minutes.

From the boat, Robert called, "Sam! Sam, can you hear me?"

Now, Sam was only moaning. Discounting much if not all of his training to follow his heart, Robert scrambled over the side of the boat where the ice was thickest. Again he began pushing the craft toward the dock. Again he plunged through the ice into water so cold it threatened to suck the very life right out of him. This time, in pulling himself back into the boat, Robert expended every ounce of strength he had. If he plunged into the water a fourth time, probably he wouldn't be strong enough to pull himself to safety.

From the boat, he called: "Sam! Sam, can you hear me?"

This time, no answer.

From shore, suddenly, Barbara shouted: "Robert! Help is coming! The 911 operator wants to speak with you . . . right now!"

By arriving at that moment, Barbara probably saved Robert's life. Instead of trying yet again to cross the ice, he responded according to his formal training: he made his way back to shore, jumped into the truck and roared back to the house. By the time he finished briefing the dispatcher, fire trucks had long since departed from Turner Valley and Black Diamond, fifteen and twenty kilometers away. Robert arrived back at the pond just behind two rescue trucks and an RCMP cruiser. Moments later, a sergeant arrived.

Sam had ceased calling for help. Three or four men were searching in the trees beyond the pond. Robert raced around the perimeter and cried: "What are you doing? He's in the water! Sam's in the water!"

From the west side, where along the shore the water lay open, Robert spotted something floating near the dock: "Look! His boots!"

Sam's skiddoo boots were bobbing on the surface of the now open water near the dock. By this time, Barbara had become completely hysterical. A team of paramedics took her back to the cottage and gave her a sedative. Our neighbour, Gail, arrived, having been alerted by the sirens. She gathered up the children, including a protesting Juli Ann, and took them back to her house three miles away.

A team of rescue workers decided to try a variation on Robert's approach. They grabbed poles and grappling hooks from a fire truck. Two of them climbed into the rowboat and, instead of pushing it from behind, began poling it forward across the ice. This took time — but it worked. Arriving beside the dock, the two men peered down into the murky water and, seeing nothing, began trying to hook Sam with their poles. They were still attempting this when a helicopter, a STARS air ambulance, arrived from Calgary, landing just inside the fence. It carried a member of the Calgary fire department aquatic rescue team, a professional diver dressed and ready to go with wetsuit, tanks, mask, flippers and personal flotation device.

Thirty minutes had elapsed since Barbara's first phone call.

The diver climbed into an aluminium boat supplied by yet another rescue team. Two other rescuers poled the boat to the dock. Immediately, the diver plunged into the freezing cold water. Visibility was zero but on his first dive, ten or fifteen feet down, he swung his arms around and struck something soft. He reached out, gathered a small, lifeless body into his arms and inflated his personal flotation device. The vest filled with air and, with Sam in his arms, the diver bobbed to the surface.

A fellow rescue worker pulled Sam onto the dock. Two men poled our son back to shore. Others placed Sam on a gurney, cut his clothes off and began trying to resuscitate him. One man cried, "I've got a heartbeat!"

Judged professionally, the rescue unfolded with textbook precision. Not a moment was lost anywhere. These highly trained professionals, including Robert, performed flawlessly. If there remained a chance to save Sam's life, these men had created it through their precise and conscientious team work. Later, they would receive a citation for their efforts. Now, rescue workers loaded Sam into the helicopter. The air ambulance had been on-site for five minutes, ten at most. Now, in a bid to save the life of our six-year-old son, it took off for Foothills Hospital.

CHAPTER FOURTEEN

GLIMPSING THE PLAN

Monday was the first day back at school after the Easter holiday. I had spoken with the three girls, one at a time, asking how they felt about returning. Without exception, they wanted to get back at it. Dawn, however, was really struggling with her grief. She asked whether I could take our youngest son, Levi, to a neighbour's for the day. Several people had offered to provide that kindness and, because I wanted to go to school with the girls, I took one of them up on it.

The flowers delivered to us during the past four days had engulfed our tiny home. We had told each girl she could pick a bouquet she liked, one that represented her feelings for Sam, and take it to school to put in the classroom. I had picked out several bouquets: some to drop off for the rescue workers at the RCMP office in Turner Valley for the valiant work the entire team had done in Sam's rescue, and another that I would drop off for Sam's peers in his kindergarten class.

I decided to begin the day with Alana in her grade-two class. The school had brought in counsellors to help the children deal with the tragedy of Sam's drowning. They were there to provide a forum for the kids to speak out and say whatever they wanted, ask whatever they wanted, and offer a completion for the children. I found myself fully involved in the process first of all with Alana.

Young children, especially those in kindergarten, grade one or grade two, have such active, vivid imaginations. After the facilitator explained briefly what had happened and asked the kids what they thought about it, one boy immediately raised his hand and said, "I have something to say! It's too bad that Sam didn't have really, really, really long legs, because he could have just walked out of the pond." Another child said, "It's too bad he couldn't have held his breath a little bit longer." A third child said, "Yeah, but he should never have gone on that ice without his Mom or Dad's permission."

The conversation went back and forth, and then the facilitator asked whether I had anything to say. The only thing I could think of saying was, "Sometimes, you kids are told not to do things by your Mom and Dad, and sometimes you might not fully understand why. Maybe you think you are smarter than Mom or Dad. That was the case with Sam. He was told not to walk on the ice, and yet he went ahead and did it, and now Sam has paid for that mistake with his life. So make sure you listen to your Moms and Dads because they really do know what's best for you."

The bell rang for the children to move to their next class. I said goodbye to Alana and moved to Laura's classroom, where I spent the same amount of time. The counsellors had already dealt with Sam's tragedy and her class had moved onto art. Laura and I spoke little; I just hung out with her. It wasn't until later that I caught a glimpse of what must have been going through Laura's mind that morning.

On weekdays, after eating breakfast with my family, I walk the girls down to the bus. One morning several months after Sam's passing, we stopped at the Quonset hut to check on the very pregnant

124

Patches. Laura cried, "Dad, look! She's having her puppies!"

Juli asked, "Dad, can we be late for school today so we can stay and watch?"

I could think of few things more educational and so said, "Yes, of course."

We all put aside our belongings and sat down in silence to observe.

One by one, the puppies were born, with Patches cleaning up immediately after each of them. Then the ever-observant Laura leaned over and, from beneath Patches, pulled out a lifeless pup still encased in its placenta: "Dad, look."

I took a pair of scissors from a nearby workbench and cut away the membrane from the pup's face. I was too late. "Laura, I'm sorry, the pup was still born."

Laura wanted to hold it, so I placed it in a clean towel and handed it to her.

She held the lifeless pup like a baby, rocked it, caressed it and quietly wept. It was a bitter-sweet, tender moment: on my right, Patches attended four mewling, newborn puppies, while on my left, Laura cradled the lone lifeless one. Wonder and harsh reality all rolled into one.

"Look, Dad!" Laura said. "It's trying to breathe!"

I drew nearer and saw that she was right: Laura's pup was opening its mouth and trying to draw breath. I said: "Keep massaging its body, Laura."

Enthusiastically, she continued, while encouraging the pup: "Come on, puppy. Come on."

Miraculously, the pup began to grunt, then squirm, then yelp.

Through tears, Laura said: "Dad, it's alive!"

Alana, Juli and I looked on in utter amazement: "Good job, Laura!"

I suggested that she give the pup to Patches for cleaning and some milk. Laura placed the pup beside

Patches, who received it with all the love and tenderness of a mother, welcoming this fifth addition to her litter. After watching for a while, I looked around and noticed that Laura had disappeared.

I found her sitting on a step, quietly weeping. Saying nothing, I sat down beside her and put my arm around her. Laura said, "I heard Sam scream."

This was unexpected, almost startling: "When Laura? In your dreams?"

"No, on the day he drowned.."

"You mean, when he went missing?"

"Yes . . . but I didn't tell anyone." These last words popped out of her mouth in an explosion of emotion and tears, like a cork popping out of a champagne bottle. She collapsed onto my lap and began sobbing aloud.

How long had she carried this secret, yearning to tell someone, feeling guilty, confused, upset? As she wept, I held her and stroked her hair. For anybody, withholding this information would have been difficult. For Laura, a sensitive nine-year-old child, it must have been an absolute torment. And so she sobbed on my lap while, just a few feet away, the new puppies suckled away at their mother.

Finally, I told Juli and Alana to go and wait in the car — that I would drive them all to school. After they had left, protesting, I took Laura's head in my hands, looked directly into her eyes and said, "Sam didn't die because you didn't tell anyone about hearing him scream. Sam died because he disobeyed Mom and Dad and walked on the ice. Do you understand?"

Still weeping, but clearly feeling considerably lighter, Laura said she understood.

We cleaned off her face and followed the other girls. Walking hand in hand towards the car, Laura said, "Dad, can I name the puppy?"

"Yes, you can," I responded.

"I want to name him Sam!"

On the first day of school after Easter, however, Laura's innocent confession lay months in the future — and I was struggling with my own emotions. Recess time arrived. I had planned to visit the staff lounge and have a coffee with the teachers, but now I didn't know if I was up to it. Maybe it wasn't such a good idea after all. I was feeling uncertain, vulnerable, almost naked, when a gregarious woman named Loraine Debman took me by the arm and said, "Come on young man, I'm going to take you inside and buy you a cup of coffee."

She pulled up a chair, sat me down, and asked me how I liked my coffee. She treated me like a favorite aunt might treat a nephew of six or seven. Frankly, I needed that. I needed her to be there. I needed her to talk directly to me. I needed her to tell me where to sit, what to do . . . to have another cookie. I needed all of those things. Loraine didn't just make conversation, though. She asked some really good questions. How was Dawn doing, was I sleeping, eating, was there anything we needed? Could she take our kids after school for a while? Did we need someone to do laundry for us? The fifteen minute break whistled by, and I said: "Thank you very much, Loraine. I really needed that."

Juli's class was my final stop. The students were starting to rehearse the play Macbeth. I remembered it from high school, grade eleven or twelve. These younger students weren't reading Macbeth in the traditional format, but had a comic book version. As I sat beside Juli in her classroom, I found myself reading and really enjoying the animated version.

The students moved into a discussion about the play. Where was MacBeth returning from? What did the witches say to him and who was King at the time? The more they discussed, the more I remembered. I even found myself feeding Juli a couple of choice answers. By the time the lunch bell rang, I had had enough. In order to be there with the kids for that morning at school, I really had to blow up my personality — to become larger that I really was. Now I felt deflated. I needed to go home. I kissed Juli, Laura, and Lana, turned on my heel and headed for home.

I didn't go straight there, however. Instead, I found myself parking the car and taking the road to the pond. Since Sam's death, I had travelled this road quite often. Now, as I walked around the pond trying to piece together the last moments that Sam had spent here, I began to sense something else at work. As I stood there, I asked myself: How would it have been possible for a person to get to Sam and rescue him? Sam had gone through the ice in mid-pond, about seventy feet from either shore. If a man tried to approach from the east, he could only walk fifteen or twenty feet before he would break through the ice, ending up in the same predicament as Sam, a considerable ways away from him and a considerable distance from shore. If the man tried to approach from the west where I now stood, he would only be able to wade into the water five or eight feet before encountering the ice, once again leaving a great distance from where Sam had fallen through.

In either scenario, how could the would-be rescuer break the ice, remain above water and work himself over to Sam before hypothermia sapped his energy. If you launched a boat onto the ice, the boat's keel would distribute the weight of the boat and the person inside of it in such a way that it would not break through the ice. Further, once inside you would have no way of propelling the boat across the ice to where Sam was.

The more that I studied the problem, the more perplexed I became — and the more I started to suspect that there might be something greater at work here. If there is such a thing as a divine plan, or God's will, it would certainly seem to have been at work on April 7th. Given the way that Sam had fallen into the pond, even a flawlessly executed rescue attempt stood little chance of succeeding.

For days and weeks after that afternoon, I tried to formulate a plan that would get both Sam and his rescuer safely out of the water. As I thought about it, I realized that any rescuer, even a mother or a father, who bravely ventured into that icy water would have suffered the same fate as Sam. On April 7, the pond water had been almost exactly zero degrees Celsius (32 Fahrenheit). At that temperature, a person can remain submerged for only a short period before the body starts to shut down in an effort to preserve vital organs and the brain. Even a vigorous adult male could only keep himself above the water for one minute, maybe two, before he would lose the use of his arms and legs.

That's when a lightning bolt of realization hit me. Young Sam, at little more than fifty pounds, dressed in blue jeans, blue jean jacket and winter skidoo boots, would have floundered for a very short period before exhaustion and hypothermia started to pull him into the arms of the awaiting angels — or, more mundanely, towards the bottom of the pond.

I remember watching footage of the rescue attempts that followed an airplane disaster in Washington, D.C. in 1982. During a January blizzard, a 737 jetliner bound for Florida crashed into a bridge over the Potomac River while taking off. Because of the icy conditions, nobody could reach the wreck from shore, but helicopter rescuers quickly arrived and dropped life vests, flotation balls and lifelines into the water. All the surviving passengers had to do was hang onto these devices to be dragged to safety — but most of them did not have enough energy left in their arms. One 50-year-old man clinging to the twisted wreck became a hero when twice he handed the lifeline to others, and then perished himself as a result of hypothermia. Out of 79 people on board, only five survived — and they were five who had been plucked from the water within minutes. They didn't have to contend with swimming through ice atop a pond, but just had to hang onto a rope.

In Northern Alberta, canoeing guides will tell you not to bother wearing a life jacket in the spring. Should you fall into the water, drowning is not the issue: hypothermia is the thief that will steal your life away. The guides call it one-minute water. Although the water is open and running, they say an average person can exist for about one minute before hypothermia begins to claim his or her life.

It was then, after trying unsuccessfully for weeks to come up with a rescue procedure, that I realized there was a greater power at work on April the seventh. That greater power had made certain that there were no other family members around — that Mom and Dad weren't aware that Sam was in the water. I began to understand that there was a better, stronger, more perfect plan in place that day, and that Sam's walking onto the pond was not just a random occurrence. Loving parents who see their children drowning don't stand on the shore and watch; they don't wait for rescue workers to show up. They have but one agenda: they plunge into the water and they don't come out until the child is safe, or until they, too, have expired....

CHAPTER FIFTEEN

MOTHER'S DAY

In the days that followed the memorial service, I developed a new rhythm. Get up early in the morning, send the girls off to school, do a few chores around the house. Then I started a process that I didn't enjoy but found necessary. People had dropped off some good books for our consumption, among them *How to Survive the Loss of a Child* by Catherine M. Sanders, *The Seat of the Soul* by Gary Zukav and *On Children and Death* by Elizabeth M.D. Kubler-Ross.

I started to read these works one chapter per sitting. Then I would go for a walk, or else sit and ponder what I had read. Often I felt very moved, especially by stories in which parents bore witness to the passing of one of their own children. Some of these stories treated a lengthy illness that a particular child had endured for six or eight months. Ultimately, after the couple had been emotionally and even financially destroyed, the child would pass away, leaving the parents with nothing.

I read stories about children who had been abducted, assaulted and then strangled to death. Another family described how their two-year-old child had wondered onto a nearby pond and fallen in, only to be discovered by the parents some two hours later. The tragedy, grief and mourning that other people had survived did not make me feel any better about the loss of my son, but did let me know that I was not alone.

Our children would come home from school and find activities to keep themselves busy. Homework included reading, spelling and math. After supper and a bath, we would send them off to bed with a story. Dawn and I remained physically present, but I knew the kids were suffering, each in her own way: they were dealing not only with the loss of their brother but with the loss of their parents' conscious presence.

The days immediately following Sam's death are a clouded blur to me now. I went from being numb and in shock to walking around like a ghost. I remember distinctly that while I was never okay, I was also never devastatingly sad — I remained somewhere agonizingly in between. The trees, the clothes and even the people around me didn't have any color to them, but seemed only shades of grey. The sky always seemed overcast and grey and even splendid greens wore a khaki hue.

I perceived no life, no vitality, no color in anything. Food lost all taste. Life itself had lost its flavor. At night, when sleep finally came, I did not sleep soundly but tossed and turned. I had read that there is an order to the grieving process: denial, bargaining, anger, depression, acceptance. I looked at this pyramid and realized that, although my son had been deceased for more than a week, I was still languishing at the bottom of the emotional chart, in shock and disbelief.

Dawn, meanwhile, was going through a totally different journey. This surprised me because I had some notion that what I was experiencing around Sam's passing was what everyone else was experiencing. But Dawn had her own insights to share and we spent a lot of time talking about what was going on. At other times, she plunged into a grief so deep and profound that all I could do was suspend my own grieving process while tending to the children and the house.

One evening in particular, I recall driving up our driveway. As I got out of the car, I heard a high-pitched, almost siren-like sound. At first I thought it must be a coyote howling. Standing by my vehicle, and paying more attention to the eerie sound, I realized it wasn't a coyote or any other animal . . . it was Dawn. But where was she? I hustled into the house, accounted for all the kids and asked Juli if everything was all right. She said yes. I asked her about Dawn and learned that she had gone to the new house, still under construction.

From inside the cabin, Dawn was not audible. But outside again, I could hear her high-pitched cry. Now that I had checked on the kids, I grew concerned for her. Should I check on her and see whether she was okay? Or should I respect her privacy and leave her alone? Eventually, I decided to do both. I climbed the hill, entered the new house and followed the sound of her voice. As I approached, I realized that she was in the room that was supposed to be Sam's.

I got a flash from two months before, remembered Dawn sitting at the dining room table in our cabin, Sam on her knee, the two of them flipping through wallpaper catalogues. Dawn would make suggestions but gave him room and allowed his personal choice to come through. Finally she turned a page and Sam exclaimed, "Wow, Mom look! It's motorcycles and racing cars . . . and they're blue!!" That was that. They picked out coordinating wall and trim colors and both were happy as clams. The "racing car" wallpaper was to become a border around the top of the room. The day before Sam fell through the ice, workmen had begun installing it.

Now, as I peered into the bedroom, I saw that

one end of the roll had not been cemented properly and was starting to peel off. And there was Dawn, down on her knees, first with her head in her hands, then with her hands clenched into fists, her head erect, her voice shouting obscenities at the dangling "race car" wall paper. I had never in my life witnessed such an emotional outpouring. Whatever thought was in her heart, Dawn howled out of her mouth, and this continued until she ran out of words. Then she would flop over onto the floor, her head in her hands, and just howl . . . .Her howl came from the deepest part of her, and put me on edge like fingernails on a chalk board, only far, far more powerfully.

Aware that this was intimate, personal time for her, I quietly left without her knowing I was there. I returned to the cottage and hid the .22 calibre rifle we kept around for skunk, vermin or coyotes that ventured too close. Was Dawn suicidal? I didn't know, but I felt my job was to keep our home as safe as I could. As I finished stowing the rifle in one corner and the ammunition in another, a neighbour arrived carrying a casserole.

I felt awkward, somewhat invaded, speaking with her on the porch. I asked her to step inside but she declined. She turned her head to one side from time to time, trying to figure out what that high-pitched noise was. Finally, having registered my knitted brow, my apprehension, with some embarrassment she identified the nature of the howl. "Tim, I know this is a difficult time for you folks," she said. "Do you want me to take the kids for a while?"

She was very sincere, and well meaning, so I measured my words and controlled my tone. I thanked her for the casserole and her concern, but noted: "The kids have a front row seat for life, death and grief right now, and I don't want them to miss a single thing."

Dawn's grief was awesome. It knew no boundaries. She just let it all out, without reservation, and without caring a bit who saw or what they thought. In the days, weeks and months that followed, I have often thought how courageous and inspiring she is as she continues her grieving. I also couldn't help thinking that not more than a generation ago, a person in her state would probably have been medicated and admitted to a hospital. What a terrible shame that would be — to feel such profound despair, have the courage to explore it, to experience its very depths, and then have someone interrupt that intimate experience with a drug, a sedative, artificial treatment or even confinement.

By now I had realized that Dawn's grieving process was entirely separate from my own. Certain aspects of it she expressed beautifully in a letter to Sam. The fall of '97, Dawn had begun volunteering at the school on Mondays. Photocopying, answering the phone, running errands — she did whatever was asked of her. About a month after Sam's passing, in an effort to re-enter her life, she returned to the school. An errand took her into Sam's kindergarten class, where the students were busy creating "Mother's Day Gifts."

The experience proved devastating. Not seeing Sam happily at work with his classmates, creating a loving gift for her — it was too much. The school secretary, Loraine Debman, noticed her and gently escorted her into an empty room. Loraine suggested that Dawn write a letter to Sam and offered to put it in the community newsletter for Mother's Day. The idea worked for Dawn and that evening, she poured her heart out on paper. Loraine wrote a brief introduction, describing Dawn's letter as "a gentle and healing message for all of us who have gone through the agony of losing a child, no matter how old or young they were. Although the incidents and actions she describes are very personal and intimate, they are also universal, a part of every day living and loving. Thank you, Dawn, for sharing your memories and reminding every one of us how precious each moment with our family is."

Under the heading "To My Son on Mother's Day," Dawn's letter followed.

My Dear Sam,

As Mother's Day approaches and I know, I see, I hear all of the children in your kindergarten class preparing for this day, I feel very hurt and very sad. I even feel anger — cheated of not having you physically here, cheated of the experience of you giving, with your beautiful sincerity, something you made for me for Mother's Day. So I write these words to you in hopes that this will ease my pain — comfort me.

Did you know how special I felt when it was me you preferred to tie your shoe laces because you liked how I did it best? Did you know how warm I felt when you asked me to help you get dressed — to put your socks on just how you liked them, to do up that difficult top button of the shirt you loved? Did you know how happy I felt when you expressed your gratitude, often several times and out of the blue, for things that you loved, like that shirt? Did you know how honored I felt when you would choose me as the person you wanted to be with: at school, at home, in the car, on the couch? Did you know how proud I felt when I would look at you and see how beautiful you were — how happy and healthy — how you lived with such passion all the time? Did you know how deeply bonded and connected to you I felt when you spoke, the admiration I felt for you for being so honest and open and clean and clear? Did you know how envious I felt — that you were a role model for me — that I wanted to be as pure and honest as you? Did you know the adoration I felt when I would get down on my knees, look you in the eyes, and tell you what a wonderful person you were?

Did you know how joyous I felt when I knew you were enjoying playing with your friends, either at home or at their places and how marvelous I felt about you experiencing your own independence? Did you know how amazed I felt when I heard you laugh, how I felt the depth and fun of who you were? Did you know how delighted I felt when I would watch you help out or play with your little brother, and I would be so pleased that you both had a brother? Did you know how much fun I felt when I would lay you down on the floor, pull up your arm and tickle you, then tickle the inside of your legs and you would laugh and laugh and ask for more? Did you know how light I felt, how I smiled inside at you making light of me being stern with you?

Did you know how vital I felt every time I sat and read a book with you, knowing I was preparing you for a world of knowledge to be obtained, sharing the pleasure of an escape into a great story? Did you know how peaceful and contented I felt when you would lay down with me for an afternoon nap, and how much love I felt when I would caress you and kiss your head as we lay together? Did you know how important I felt when you came to me for comforting when you were hurt and how good I felt to hold you until you felt better?

Did you know how good I felt when I washed your clothes and bedding and hung them in the sunshine and fresh air to dry? And how appreciated I felt when you snuggled into bed at night and told me how good it smelled? Did you know how my heart was melting when at bedtime you would hug and kiss me so hard and say "That's how much I love you!" and then you would say, "You're the best Mom I ever had!"? Did you know how compassionate I felt when you would finally settle enough from enjoying life to realize that you were hungry and I would make you a peanut butter and jam sandwich with chocolate chips in it because I knew that you not only wanted it but needed it?

Did you know how awed I felt when you would be sitting on the couch, and I would be standing in the kitchen and you would say, "Mom, I'm touching you right now because I'm touching the couch, the couch is touching the floor, this floor is touching your floor and you're touching that floor too!" Momentarily my breath was taken away because I used to think that very same way. Did you know how inspired I felt when you would ask me about every single piece of garbage you had and if it belonged in the "recycles"? How your caring about the environment inspired me to care even more?

Did you know how assured and confident I felt when I nurtured my own needs, knowing I was teaching you to do the same and how amazed I felt when I realized how much you loved yourself — just by the way your love for others and for life was given and received? Did you know how wholesome and complete I felt when I would look at you and your sisters and brother and your Dad and I would feel the beauty of my family and think "My dreams have come true — I have everything"?

Did you know how shocked, shattered, sad, numb, devastated, alone, lonely, empty, helpless, hopeless, hurt, angry, upset, wounded, damaged, fragile, confused, lost, sick, outraged, depressed, abandoned, cheated, anguished, afraid, humbled, heart-broken, disbelieving, unaccepting, yet completely understanding and accepting I felt when you died?

Oh, dear Sam, how I miss you.

In living, you gave me the opportunity to experience the giving and receiving of unconditional love. In dying, you have given me the opportunity to experience the most intense passion of unconditional love — through the depths of sorrow. Before you died, I knew I had everything because I had love. I know now that I still have everything — unconditional love for myself, for others, for life, forever. Did your know how blessed and grateful I felt every moment of every day to have you as my son? Thank you Sam for the most incredible Mother's Day gift I have ever received!

CHAPTER SIXTEEN

THE FINAL SOLUTION

Some corporations expect that if a loved one passes away on Friday, you're to bury them on Saturday, grieve on Sunday and return to work on Monday. The way that I've set up my business, and given the incredible competency of my right-hand man, manager Don Campbell, I was able to take an extended period of time off to deal with the personal issues that arose out of Sam's passing.

I contacted Don at the office to discuss some business matters, like paying Revenue Canada taxes that had come due. There were some other minor issues as well, but I asked Don if he could handle them until I felt like getting back in the saddle. He said no problem. If I relayed certain information, he would look after the rest of it. This was a luxury and I knew it.

While I was talking to Don on the telephone, I felt energized and worth while. However, as soon as I hung up the telephone, memories of Sam and the things we used to share forced themselves back into my consciousness. On top of the TV lay the stereo headphones I had bought for Sam. Often, while still in play school, he would make his way down to the office in the mornings.

Invariably, he wanted to watch something like *Toy Story*, *Space Jam* or *Batman Returns*. The problem was, when I was speaking to a client on the phone, the volume had to be so low that Sam couldn't hear the TV. At a mall one day, I found the answer at Radio Shack. Now, as I looked at the headphones, I recalled how I had enjoyed Sam coming into the office. How I enjoyed wrapping him in a blanket in front of the fire place. How I enjoyed just being around him, even if he was in his own world and I was in mine. I also realized how immensely I would miss his silent presence.

I became depressed, and that depression lasted the rest of the day. I felt very down, very alone. Shortly after supper, when Dawn and I got a moment together, I suggested that maybe later we could make love. If I had thrown a bucket of ice cold water on her, I wouldn't have gotten a more startled look. Aghast, she said, "What are you talking about? I just lost my son and now you want to have sex? I don't want you near me! I don't want you touching me! I don't want anything to do with you, I want space...."

In my foolishness, I asked her how long she expected that time to last, and when I might dare to again bring up the topic. She said, "Tim, I have to learn to live without my son for the rest of my life. I can certainly live without sex for the rest of my life, too." With that, she spun on her heel, went into the bedroom and closed the door.

Didn't she realize that I had been carrying the ball since April 8? Giving her space and looking after the majority of the heaviest challenges? Was I so out of line? I felt my depression intensify. I had nowhere to go, no place to hide. I felt sorry for myself. By now, the kids were getting ready for bed. My wife was not in any mood to talk with me or offer me any kind of consolation. She had her own issues to deal with. I found myself walking out to the car and driving to the nearest liquor store. I bought a bottle of scotch with a view to ridding myself, as quickly as possible, of all these thoughts and emotions.

I sat in the car and poured myself a stiff one. The first drink made me feel warm and fuzzy. The second made me feel better than I had felt in a month. By the third drink I was feeling very little pain. I drove to a motel, checked in and turned on the television. I found a depressing drama and watched it, continuing to drink until I felt nothing at all. Eventually, I fell into a fitful sleep.

Over the next few weeks, I repeated this destructive behaviour. Soon, I was going drinking every second day. One day I would feel fine and the next depression would set in and I would drink to alleviate it. The trouble with drinking to relieve depression is that alcohol is a mood-altering substance — one that, in most people, causes feelings of depression. I was no exception. I drank because I was depressed, and the more I drank the more depressed I became.

Anyone familiar with alcoholism knows the vicious cycle. Inevitably, I spiralled downwards. During one of these drunken evenings, I started to feel that there was no hope for me, no way out. I was sinking deeper and deeper and deeper into a black hole, and no matter where I looked, all I could see was darkness.

My reluctance, my refusal to engage my grief over Sam, spawned something in me that was very dark and extremely ugly. In truth, I could no longer bear the pain of Sam's loss . . . I longed to be released from it. I decided that the only way out of this living hell was to take my own life. My dark side had just shifted into high gear . . . and so I drank. And as I drank, I elaborated the perfect plot. When my dark side is involved, my ego is involved — and my ego said, "You can't just go out and take your own life. You have to make it look like an accident. Suicide looks cowardly, but an accident? That is tragic and demands sympathy."

The best way to proceed, I decided, was to stage a car accident. Just before sunset, I would drive west along a two-lane highway so that the excuse for the accident would be unmistakable: "Well, the sun was in his eyes. He couldn't see the oncoming traffic." I would wait for a large truck and turn out directly into its path. The oncoming truck would be travelling sixty-five miles an hour and I would be travelling the same, for a combined impact speed of one hundred and thirty miles an hour. I also knew that modern vehicles had air bags, fenders, engines and hoods that, upon impact, crumpled in a pre-engineered fashion to protect the driver.

With that in mind, I decided to use my 1972 Chevy pick-up truck. It was constructed long before any technological safety advantages even existed. This would ensure that I wouldn't spend any time in a coma, or in an intensive care ward: my death would be instantaneous. By taking on a large truck, I also knew the other driver would not be injured (at least not physically). I would make sure that my seatbelt was on, to further weight the argument of "accidental death" (as if a seatbelt would have any bearing whatsoever on the outcome of such an accident).

Over the next few wretched nights, while drinking heavily, I elaborated this plan. I concluded that the best way to set this up so the other vehicle couldn't swerve out of my way was to wait until the oncoming truck was driving into a right turn. That would mean that the majority of the weight, velocity and motion would be moving directly towards me. For the oncoming driver, getting out of the way would be almost impossible. I reasoned that, if possible, I should come up behind a vehicle driving in my lane with my turn indicator on, so that at the last minute I could swing out and collide with the oncoming eastbound truck. This would ensure that the other vehicle wouldn't have a chance to dodge me. The total velocity would be enough to achieve my goal and the investigating constables would chalk up my death to driver error, not suicide.

Finally, I resolved to act. I checked my life insurance policy, noted that all payments were current and the two-year suicide restriction had long since expired. My mind was clear and lucid. I felt better knowing that all my pain and suffering would soon be over. Then, as the sun began to set, doubts began popping into my mind. How would the driver in the other vehicle feel? How would my friends feel? And my remaining children? How would they feel, growing up without having their natural father around for baseball, basketball, swimming, hockey, horse riding, family picnics, for the Christmas pageants, the graduations. How would Dawn feel? The more that I thought about it, even in my befuddled state, the more I realized that it was a damn good plan, but maybe I should work out a couple of minor wrinkles. Instead of acting, I checked into a motel room and drank until I passed out . . . .

The next morning I rose early, had coffee and breakfast at a local cafe and headed home long before anyone was out of bed. I took a shower, brushed my teeth and prepared breakfast for the kids. Dawn took one look at me and said, "What's with you?"

"Nothing, why?"

"Because you look pretty rough. Your eyes are baggy and bloodshot . . . have you been drinking?"

I brushed her off with a joke: "Only to extremes."

That day, while sitting in my office, I found myself remembering my youth. My Dad did two jobs and worked fourteen hours a day from Monday to Friday. He was never around on weekday evenings except, of course, for Fridays. As soon as he arrived home on Friday night, he would start to drink. He wouldn't stop until Sunday night, when he would invariably be found in his E-Z Boy recliner, in front of the T.V.,

145

passed out. Monday morning he would get up, shower, shave and head off to work.

Apparently, he was the model employee, and sober as a judge until the next Friday night. This pattern played itself out over and over again. My father, the ultimate escape artist. My mother, on the other hand, was a tea-totaller. When she wasn't over-compensating for my my father's mental and physical absence, she was covering up, dutifully cooking, cleaning and taking care of him. Although she was almost always there physically, she was often mentally and emotionally unavailable.

As I sat in my office I realized that, without consciously being aware of it, I had fallen into my parents' most dark and destructive patterns. During the day, I tended to Dawn and the kids, ensuring that the house and finances were in order — like my mother. During the evening, I withdrew into an alcoholic fog and drifted in never-never land until I was needed again — like my father. In both states, I remained totally shut down. I was hiding from the tidal wave of emotion that had arisen from my son's death and threatened to swamp me. I was unwilling to wade into it. Even now I have trouble admitting it, but the truth is: I was afraid.

This must have been the point, I realized, that my father reached in the summer of 1975, when I was sixteen. He must have looked at his miserable, unrealized life and decided it wasn't worth living any more. He remained disconnected from his wife and children — those who were supposed to be nearest him. He had lost all hope of fulfilling the dreams of his youth. He could no longer deny the mountainous backlog of hard, emotional work that cried out for his attention. Unwilling to open up, unable to confront his dark side and wrestle it into submission, my father took his life on July 8, 1975.

I distinctly remember feeling very little for my

father at his funeral. To me, he had been a closed book. During our sixteen years together, living in the same house, I could think of few experiences we had shared....

That night, for the first time in a long time, when depression came calling, I resisted. With Dawn and the kids in bed, I lay on the couch in the front room. I twitched and whimpered like an eight-week-old pup separated from its mother for the first time. Away from the warmth and comfort of my alcoholic nipple, I felt the night pushing hard, bringing memories of playing, wrestling and laughing with Sam.

I trembled, I shook and I wept. Engulfed by grief, I could see no end to the sadness and heartache that lay ahead. I awoke from a vivid nightmare in a cold sweat and in total darkness. For the longest time, I had no idea where I was. In the nightmare, Sam had just fallen through the ice and was screaming for me to rescue him. I was so drunk, I couldn't move. Finally, after struggling to the hole in the ice where Sam had fallen in, I pulled out my son's lifeless body.

Now, sitting up on the couch, shaking after my horrible dream, I felt more frightened and alone than I had ever felt. I had made a conscious decision to face my emotions but now I felt overwhelmed — utterly swamped. The emotional waves rolled over me, battering me like I was a rudderless, ten-foot aluminum boat adrift on the ocean in a hurricane.

Looking back, I recognize this as the lowest point I ever experienced.

I see also that it was a turning point.

CHAPTER SEVENTEEN

SYMBOLS OF TRANSFORMATION

The next morning, after the kids went off to school, I headed to my office in the Quonset hut. It was time to work on me. I began identifying my patterns by writing them out on paper. The grief would start to push in on me. Rather than deal with it, I would try to escape. I would escape the grief through work, alcohol or, by far the most dominant, caretaking. As I looked after my wife and children, and tackled the day-to-day chores of the house, I would seek acknowledgment for my sacrifice.

By late evening, when recognition hadn't come, I would numb out by drinking. This would hold my grief at bay. But alcohol is a depressant. The more I drank, the more depressed I became. The more depressed I became, the sorrier I felt for myself and the more I wanted to end my miserable, pathetic existence. The following morning the vicious cycle would begin all over again, as I continued to avoid facing my unprocessed feelings about the death of Sam.

Once I had identified the ugly, self-destructive pattern, I got out a pillow and a plastic baseball bat. I wanted cathartically to release my pent-up emotions. I beat the pillow, at first with no emotion. Then, from the deepest part of me, came all the anger, dread, shame and agony associated with the pattern that was making me feel so terrible. After ten minutes of pillow pounding, I broke into a light sweat; after twenty, a lather; and after thirty, liquid was running down my body, a combination of alcohol, sweat, anxiety, anger and depression.

When finally I had exhausted every ounce of energy I had, I dropped the plastic bat and flopped down onto the pillow, panting heavily. I felt a tingling in my body, a tingling in my chest — a tingling that said, "You've done good work," a tingling that said, "There's hope," a tingling that said, "You're alive!"

I closed my eyes and, remembering the Hoffman Process, asked a question: "What am I to do now?" I imagined something in my right hand. In my mind's eye, I drew my hand across my heart and, when I opened it (still with my eyes closed) I envisioned a butterfly. One thing I have come to realize about my symbols is that they represent something to me and only me. If I work at it a while, I will understand what a given symbol means — as with the picnic table. In this case, I had no idea what the butterfly might mean. To me, the symbol was so obscure that I discounted it as meaningless, gave up grappling and decided to go for a long walk.

As I walked, almost despite myself, I kept opening and closing my hand — and every time I did so, in my mind's eye, a butterfly flew out. The butterfly I envisioned, quite specifically, was brown with a thread of white that ran along the outside of its wings, about an eighth of an inch from the edge. Every time I opened and closed my hand, the symbol would reappear. I was stymied. I knew nothing of this butterfly or any other, and I thought the symbol particularly strange because at this time of year, there were no butterflies anywhere.

Continuing my walk, I glanced down — and to my astonishment discovered a dozen or so caterpillars attempting to cross the road. In my mind, a flash of lightening crackled across darkness. I knew, of course, that if they survived, these caterpillars would turn into butterflies. From down the road a pickup truck was speeding towards me. Instantly, I became a crazed madman, crying aloud: "I must save them!"

Obviously, if the pickup truck drove over this highway when a dozen or more caterpillars were crossing, several of them would get run over. If that happened, they would never complete their transformation into something far more beautiful than what they currently were. I had to get those caterpillars off the road!

Furiously, I began gathering caterpillars, running to the far side of the road (where they were going) and gently tossing them into the ditch. I moved as fast as I could but realized that more and more caterpillars were emerging onto the near side of the road. Even so, I managed to clear the necessary lane of caterpillars and stood and watched the vehicle pass. I then entered the ditch on the near side of the highway, harvested as many "furry friends" as I could and delivered them to the other side. I spent the next hour serving as an unofficial caterpillar crossing guard.

That evening, sitting in my office, I reflected on this experience. I felt that a significant message was being communicated to me. One of the most incredible transformations on earth is that from caterpillar to butterfly. Clearly, the butterfly represented Sam. He had expired as a human being, and yet he continued to live — a soul who had transformed himself into a spirit, a beautiful spirit, a spirit that could now fly instead of crawl.

The butterfly was also an earthly challenge. I had to change my life and right now. I was still in the caterpillar state, a human being who had not yet evolved. I had to make a transition — to grow. Even as I thought this, I felt a rush and, in my imagination, felt another lightning bolt go through me. This surge reminded me to feel a reverence for life — a reverence that recognized all life must be preserved, all life must be respected, all life is here for a purpose.

As I pondered further, I realized that the message for me was, "My life is important." Yes, a terrible thing had happened. Yes, it was going to take a long time to get over — but my life was important. My life was important to my family and my friends; even more than that, my life was important, as everyone's is, in the universal pattern of transformation.

That night I had a dream. This dream was so vivid that, when I awoke, I went into the kitchen and wrote it down right away. The setting was surreal. In the sparse clouds above our home in Millarville sits a set of bleachers like those you would see behind home plate at any baseball diamond in any playground in North America. On the first rung of the bleachers sits my natural father, dressed casually and watching events unfold below him. He is alert and attentive to everything going on in my home.

Without being told, I know that my father, who committed suicide, is in what Christians might call purgatory. Somehow, I understand that my father must watch his loved ones face and pass the challenges that defeated him in his lifetime. He must bear witness as his family members struggle with their own realities. Once he has witnessed our lives (his purgatory sentence, if you will), then and only then will he be allowed to re-enter the human experience with a new contract to evolve.

So there sits my father, "witnessing" my daily plight as I struggle with suicide and grief, sometimes withdrawing, sometimes at peace. Always he is witnessing, hoping, praying and rooting for us to triumph and advance so we can all move forward, so all may evolve. As my father "witnesses" with

152

his careful eye, my son Samuel Jess arrives and takes a spot on a riser above him and to his right. My son looks the way I remember him on April 6th: short hair, blue jeans, blue jean jacket, his favorite T-shirt and running shoes. "Hi, Grandad," he says to my father.

My father turns to him, more calm and grounded than I remember him, and says, "Hi, kiddo."

Sam asks, "How are they doing today?"

"Well, they are all moving ahead today. It's really a delight to watch. The butterfly was a nice touch."

The two of them watch intently for a while.

Eventually, Sam says, "Well, Grandad, I'll see you later."

They hug and the image fades. Once again I understand that my son can move around the spirit world at ease because he fulfilled his contract yes, full-filled. He is a free spirit, an old spirit at ease and totally okay.

My father, on the other hand, would appear to have a karmic debt to repay — one that involves his daily witnessing of my family and his family. However, both Sam and my father share the same active need. Both need me, need all of us, to move ahead, to evolve, to full-fill our lives. Along with all the other spirits, they are pulling for us here on earth.

Now, whenever I'm struggling, when I'm pushed to the limits, I look into those bleachers and call for their strength, love and support. Always, I find solace — sometimes in witnessing a sunset, other times seeing a fawn with its mother or else just interacting with caterpillars. Are these symbols created by God, by Allah, by the interconnected universe . . . or by my own imagination? It hardly matters. I enjoy the thought that my son Sam personally creates them and sends them to help me, to guide me, and then sits back in the bleachers and watches, and smiles, and laughs . . . and cries.

For the next week to ten days, caterpillars continued to appear in my life. They showed up on the highway, on the bed spread, on the shower curtain and the kitchen counter. They showed up in my briefcase, they showed up here, there and everywhere. They drove home the message, over and over and over again, that I am a caterpillar, and I had better look after myself as a caterpillar because something beautiful lies ahead. I can't see it yet, but it's there, just beyond the next transformation.

The week after the caterpillars, my business required attention. I traveled 300 km north to Edmonton to address some details around a problem property I had bought in the fall of 1998. It wasn't physically laborious work, but it required my full and undivided attention. As it happened, Don Campbell and I had to work side by side. The two of us, as a team, identified the issues, categorized them and then tackled them one by one. At the end of the day, we ate a good dinner and retired to our rooms.

I watched a light-hearted movie and enjoyed it thoroughly. After logging my wake-up call, I sat reflecting on the day and realized that, for the first time in a long time, for however briefly, today I had felt worthwhile, needed. I had laughed and, in a modest way, enjoyed myself — an experience that, since the passing of my son, I had thought vanished forever.

CHAPTER EIGHTEEN

SPORTS AND BUTTERFLIES

Sports have always played an important role in my life. As a boy growing up in Calgary, I devoted half my waking hours to physical activities. The local outdoor hockey rink, "Tuxedo Park," was just two blocks from my home, and there I spent countless evenings and weekends playing shinny hockey (pick-up games). After my father had passed away, I was fortunate enough, at age seventeen, to earn a three-year bursary at Notre Dame College in Wilcox, Saskatchewan. There I completed my high school and two years of university while playing numerous sports including hockey for Père Murray's famous "Hounds." Later, in Edmonton, while attending the Northern Alberta Institute of Technology, I played defence with a team that won the national small-college championship.

When the kids got old enough to play sports, naturally I started coaching. In January of 1999, I had volunteered to coach Millarville's under-nine soccer team. This was to be a dream come true. I knew that Laura and Alana, nine and seven respectively, would play on that team. I also felt that I could bring Sam up, from his league, to play. He was feisty enough and more than willing to get his nose dirty. I looked forward to having three of the five kids on the same team — on our team.

Three weeks after Sam passed, Brian Siray, the coordinator for the Millarville Soccer Program, called. He expressed regret over the recent loss of my son and said he would understand if I didn't wish to coach this year. If I wished to withdraw, no problem: somebody else had agreed to take over the under-nines — but only if I wished. Lately, I hadn't thought much about coaching and I asked for a little time to decide.

I found myself remembering how Sam loved sports. One day when he was about three, as we walked through a sports store, he spotted a pint-size basketball hoop. Sam quickly found the accompanying ball and we spent the next half hour playing hoops in the aisle. Sam loved it so much that, when the salesman came over and asked if he could help us. I said, "Sure, we'll take the whole shooting match."

At this time, we were still living in Edmonton. Sam's three sisters were all in school and after his mid-day nap he would often drag Ester, our all-time favorite nanny, out onto our driveway for a "hoop fest." I had set the height of the basket at five feet. This was a bit challenging for Sam, but I remember how impressed he was that Ester at four foot nine could slam dunk just like Michael Jordan, his favorite basketball star.

I had purchased a house kitty corner from our home and converted it into my office. There, I would work away until "the game" broke out and often linger at my window admiring the bond between Sam and Ester. Sam was tireless and would continue to play by himself long after Ester went inside to prepare supper. As the months passed, Sam continued to enjoy his basketball games, playing either with Ester, his older sisters or myself. By the age of four, he was dribbling with both hands and doing lay-ups from either side of the basket (and sometimes sinking them).

Some afternoons at around three, after Sam and

Ester finished their game, he and I would walk out to meet his three sisters returning from school. We would meet halfway at the 7-Eleven convenience store, and there on the curb we would play another kind of game — the M&M World Championship. Like most parents, when our kids asked for snacks, Dawn and I tried hard to coax them away from sugar and towards fruit. The M&M-candy game was a compromise.

Shortly after arriving at the convenience store, I would purchase one small bag of M&M's to be shared by all five of us. Sitting in a row on the curb, I would start the game by putting an M&M in Sam's ear. If he correctly guessed the color, he could fish it out and eat it. If he guessed wrong, I got to fish it out and eat it. Then Sam would put an M&M in Laura's ear and invite her to guess. So it went, round and round, until it came back to Juli putting an M&M in my ear. The kids enjoyed all this tremendously.

Other times, instead of sitting on the curb, we would carry the bag of M&M's home and play in the cool green grass of our front lawn while watching the clouds roll past overhead. It was there that a different version of the game was born. The guessers, instead of having the M&Ms placed in their ears, had them placed on their closed eyelids. This allowed a new rule to be introduced. The closed eye had to remain closed, but the guesser was allowed to open the other eye and "cheat" by looking. This, of course, was physically impossible, but it encouraged guessers to contort their faces and cross their eyes, much to the hilarity of everybody else.

After a few practice rounds, the championship would begin. Each guesser was accorded ten M&M's. Alana one day went nine for ten, her only wrong pick being purple (M&M doesn't make a purple). In any event, after a grand champion had been determined, all contestants were obliged to drink a full glass of water and eat a piece of fruit. The champion's reward was bragging rights until next time, plus the chance to eat the few remaining M&Ms.

Remembering all this as I sat in my office, I called back Brian Siray and told him that I still wanted to coach — but I would prefer to co-coach with whoever he had found to replace me. This suited him fine.

Before the first practice, to set goals and objectives, I got together a couple of times with my fellow coach, a woman named Penny. We shared the view that the experience the kids were going to have playing soccer was more important than whether they won or lost. They should have a positive experience. We decided to set up our drills, practices and games to make them fun and inclusive. We would use frozen tag as a warm-up and cross-over games like three-legged soccer (two children would tie their legs together) to teach coordination and team work.

Before practice, with a view to leaving a lasting impression, I would go to the store and buy a couple of bags of ice and two dozen soft drinks. I would put these into a cooler so that, at the end of the practice, the kids could pick out a Coke or a Seven-Up and hang around for a while. For some kids under nine, having a cold drink after practice is the essence of the soccer experience.

On the first day of practice, while I was laying out the equipment, a young boy walked over to me and said, "Look! Look at my finger." I looked and there on his finger sat a butterfly — a brown butterfly with a white ribbon of colour edging its wings. The creature was identical to the one I had seen a few weeks earlier in my symbol trips. The boy said: "Isn't it gorgeous? This is the first butterfly I've seen this year."

The boy was so excited and expressive that the other children and even the parents gathered around to see the first butterfly of the season. I was glad they were all paying close attention to this butterfly, because there I stood, just a few feet away, weeping like a child. I couldn't say why, exactly. But clearly, the butterfly was a symbol. It was crucially important for me that I was involved in a transformation, whether I understood it completely or not — and that transformation was symbolized by the butterfly.

The butterfly stayed on this young man's finger for the longest time. Finally, Coach Penny decided to get the soccer practice under way. The butterfly started to fly away and I felt emotionally torn between wanting to stay at the practice and following the butterfly. My intellect was again battling my emotions: I knew that I was obligated to remain with the kids but the little boy inside me wanted to chase the butterfly. The little boy inside me, captivated, wanted to go with that butterfuly as it flew farther and farther away.

I stood on the sidelines with my clipboard, pretending I was recording names. Really, I was hiding my face as the tears continued to fall. At last, instead of trying to escape, I was allowing my heart to open and, even more importantly, I was allowing myself to feel — feel the loss of my son, feel the depth of my sadness, and begin my long and uncharted grieving process. I gave careful and sincere thanks for the life I was still living.

CHAPTER NINETEEN

VISIONS OF SAM

My eldest daughter Juli, now ten, had chosen to play baseball that spring. One evening, she was playing a game in Millarville and Dawn, still feeling that she didn't want to go out in public, had asked if I would take her alone. It was a beautiful spring evening. On arriving, I took a position where I would be close to the other parents but wouldn't enter into conversation. That just seemed comfortable for me these days — to be able to watch and enjoy my children and not enter into too much idle chit-chat. Juli had a couple of hits and made some good plays.

Then, typically for Southern Alberta in the springtime, heavy, dark storm clouds began to roll in. A few lightning bolts struck and, because the kids were holding aluminum bats, the umpire consulted the coaches and called the game. I hung around and helped the team gather up equipment, and then, as the rain began, started walking with Juli, hand-in-hand, towards the parking lot. Johnny's mother hadn't shown up yet, so we invited him to climb into our vehicle. Soon the rain was pounding down. After a few minutes, Johnny's mother pulled into the parking lot and away he went.

As I pulled onto the dirt road that led to the highway, the rain eased. At the highway, I looked both ways to make sure no traffic was coming and spotted a butterly fluttering up, up, up towards an absolutely spectacular rainbow. The rainbow was so incredible that I put the vehicle in park to get out and observe it. I've always believed that if I found the end of the rainbow, there I would find a pot of gold.

As the rain slowed and almost stopped, Juli pointed to the right: "Look Dad! You can see where the rainbow touches down." Sure enough, in a pasture immediately before us, the rainbow touched down. Juli and I ran to where it did so and spent a few minutes looking around for gold. Prismatic, multi-colored light sparkled and shimmered all around us. I felt totally energized. Looking back at the soccer pitch, I saw the other end of the rainbow. This was the first time I had ever seen a double-ended rainbow. It was breathtaking. As the sun split the cloud cover, increasing the illumination, I could only marvel.

As Juli and I stood there in wonder, a second rainbow began to form immediately in front of the first. It started to the left of the pasture and arched over to touch the school where Sam's memorial service had been held. At that I felt so moved I started to weep. We stood in the pasture for many moments, until the sun emerged completely from behind the clouds and started breaking up the rainbow.

Juli and I said little as we drove home. On arrival, however, we behaved like pre-school children competing to tell their mother the same story. The rainbows had been truly awesome. I was so full of wonder and gratitude that I found myself retiring early, having spent an entire evening, the first since Sam's death, feeling good about myself and my surroundings. I entertained no negative thoughts, felt no grief, battled no lingering heartache. As I drifted off to sleep, I remained charged with the sighting of the double rainbow.

That night, I dreamed again about my son. I was walking down the long road towards the pond, taking the same route that Sam had taken on that fateful day. In my dream, Sam appeared before me looking much the same as our last day together. He had short cropped brown hair and wore Levi blue jeans, a Levi jean jacket and his special runners with a blue stripe. He was calm, had a twinkle in his eye and smiled his patented smile. I blurted, "Son, it's so good to see you."

He said, "Dad, it's really good to see you too — but I can't stay long."

His manner was more refined and sophisticated than I remembered, but his warmth was there in spades. I said, "Why is that?" I was puzzled: why would he have only a bit of time? He replied, "Because I've got somewhere else I have to go — but I do have some time for you."

I found looking at him and talking with him so immensely satisfying. I felt calm and at ease right down to my soul. "Sam," I said, "there's something that's been bothering your mother and me since the accident. We can't understand why you went out on the ice after we warned you so many times not to go. How come you went?"

As I said the words, the question gnawed at my insides. Beyond all questions I had about the events of the day, that one, the why, was the ultimate question. He said, "I went out there 'cause I was thirsty, Dad."

In my dream state, the words he spoke took on great weight. I understood that Sam had been thirsty, but not for water — that he was thirsty for the other side. He was speaking of a thirst for knowledge of the world beyond. I looked into his eyes. Neither of us spoke. His eyes had become a window to the wisdom of the universe and I felt highly energized. I said: "Son, what did you enjoy most here on earth?"

With boyish enthusiasm, he responded, "Dad, I love my family. It's such a cool family. I just wanted to come back and tell you that it's okay — that I'm just fine, Dad . . . and I love you guys very much."

As the vision of Sam faded away, I awoke. Of course I wanted to write down everything I could remember, so I swung out of bed and headed for the kitchen to fetch pen and paper, pulling on my bathrobe as I went. Suddenly, I had a feeling I was being watched. To my left, my peripheral vision picked up a figure standing in the doorway of the children's bedroom. As I turned to look more closely, the figure retreated into the bedroom. Although I did not see the face, I saw a person about four feet tall, wearing a blue jean jacket and matching jeans — a person with short brown hair and also wearing white cotton socks.

It must be Alana, I told myself. Alana was about the same size as Sam, and she had gotten into the habit of donning Sam's clothes when she missed him. As I approached the doorway, guided by my intellect, I decided that Alana, dressed in Sam's clothes, must have heard me get up and stepped to the doorway to see what was happening.

Quickly entering the children's bedroom, I found all three girls in bed beneath the covers. It struck me that neither Alana nor any of the other kids could have been in the doorway one second and under the covers in the next. I would have heard the rustling of the sheets, the creaking of the mattress. One girl's eyes must be blinking in an effort to persuade me that she was asleep. My intellect protested, wanting proof. I delicately pulled back the sheets one by one to find three pajama-clad children all in a deep state of slumber.

As I stood up, trying to find a logical explanation for what I had seen, I caught a hint of something…an aroma. I have always been able to tell each of my children's clothes, not by the size or color, but by the faint personal scent that stays with the item, even after washing. The scent I smelled now was Sam's. I knew this without a doubt and instantly my intellect fell silent. Feeling now that Sam's spirit might still be in the house, I quietly moved from room to room, gently calling his name — but Sam was gone. The feeling that stayed with me following the dream and the sighting was so wonderful that I sat down at the counter and, through joyful tears, tried to capture the whole experience on paper.

After I had laid my pen down, I remained filled with wonder. I sat for more than an hour, just savoring what I had experienced. As morning broke, into the kitchen wandered a groggy, sleepy-eyed Alana. She pulled the quilt off the couch and settled onto my knee for a cuddle. Rocking easily back and forth, she broke the silence: "Dad, I had a dream about Sam last night."

Cloaking my excitement as best I could, I replied, "Tell me about it."

She said, "I went into your's and Mom's bedroom and Sam was sitting on Mom's side of the bed watching her sleep."

"Did you talk to him?"

"No, but he said something to me." I waited in silence for a million years before she continued. "He said . . . "Tell Dad I'm okay and tell Mom I really like her flowers.'"

Eventually, I inquired: "Anything else?"

"I think so Dad, but I can't remember." She took a beat, then added matter-of-factly: "Sam says to tell you he's okay . . . . will you make me some breakfast?"

That was that. With Alana, it's best to let her be. When and if she remembered more, I knew she would bring it to me. Now I was certain that Sam had visited last night, one way or another. The message that he gave to Alana was, for me, a very powerful one. Somewhere deep inside me, a wound had been festering, unhealed: "Is my boy okay?" Both my own dream and Alana's reported the same succinct message from Sam: "I'm okay." The message was short but unbelievably powerful and effective. The words soothed my soul and allowed healing to begin at last.

In the days following Sam's passing, the flower arrangements had arrived by the dozens. Eventually, Dawn had phoned the flower shop and told them, "Please don't deliver any more — our cabin is jammed to the ceiling. Kindly ask that people make contributions in lieu of flowers either to STARS Air Ambulance or the Children's Wish Foundation.

As I've already mentioned, when the children went back to school, Dawn invited each of them to bring an arrangement to their class. Also, she told me to drop off bouquets for the rescue workers. I felt certain that this was what Sam had been referring to — the way Dawn had lovingly distributed the flowers.

When Dawn joined us for breakfast, Alana shared her story with her. At first Dawn seemed puzzled, but then she went about her routine. Later that day, I asked if Sam's message was indeed about the giving away of arrangements and the donations in lieu of flowers. She paused and said, "No . . . I don't think so." She went on to explain: "One day following Sam's passing, I was at a nursery. Some yellow and purple pansies caught my eye. They looked like flowers Sam would like. I bought them, then returned home and planted them in the flower beds to remind me of his love and energy. While I was on my knees, arranging them, I kept thinking to myself, through tears, 'These are for you, son.' I felt like I was doing something loving for Sam."

"Dawn, did you ever tell Alana that?"

"No, Tim. That's the funny thing. I've never told anyone . . . ."

CHAPTER TWENTY

SUMMER AT THE SHUSHWAPS

When the kids get out of school at the end of June, usually we would spend a couple of days around home and then head for the Shushwap Lakes in British Columbia. We had discovered these lakes, located a six-hour drive west of Calgary, about five years before, when we had taken a two-week vacation. The next year we took three weeks, and each year after that we extended our stay. In the summer of 1998, we had rented a place for five weeks.

For the summer of 1999, we started cottage-hunting late and couldn't find accommodation for longer than one week. The more ads we ran, the more people we talked to, the clearer it became. I began to believe the universe was sending me a message: this year, the Johnsons get to spend only one week in the Shushwaps. After that, your presence is required elsewhere. We swallowed our disappointment, loaded up our vehicle and headed out.

Although we have four surviving children, making six of us in total, I felt the absence of Sam intensely — lying on the beach, walking in the woods, riding in the boat, I felt this terrible void. Sam was an unbelievably energetic, rambunctious kid. At the Shushwaps, from dawn until dusk, he would play non-stop — running, jumping, swimming, building sand castles or, with his siblings, tubing behind our motor boat. Some time after supper, maybe around the campfire, he would simply fall asleep on the person next to him. Sam would expend every ounce of energy he had. When he was tired, that was it: he didn't have the energy to stumble back to the condo and crawl into bed, but would simply fall asleep where he was.

In 1999, the first few days at the Shushwaps were especially difficult as fond memories flooded me. I kept remembering the previous summer, when with Sam we had arrived on a hot, sunny day and immediately got our motorboat into the water. Soon all hands were on deck, clad only in bathing suits and life jackets, ready to go. Five minutes later, as we cruised along with the wind in our hair and the sun on our backs, one glance at the children's faces delivered the unanimous verdict: there's no place in summer like the Shushwaps.

Here you find sunning, swimming, golfing, water skiing, tubing, afternoon siestas, barbecues, camp fires, marsh-mellow roasts, ice-cream stands, dinners out — the perfect climax to a hectic school year. Many afternoons, when the sun was high and as the temperature peaked, we would find ourselves on the water, cruising with our clan and various new friends from the adjoining cottages.

Not every memory was a fond one, of course. After lunch one day, Dawn and the children went to the adjoining park. I lay down on the couch to catch a few winks before we headed out on the water. I was just nodding off when I heard a muffled, "Open the door." It was Dawn. "Tim, help me!"

Her tone was so frantic that, in a heartbeat, I reached the door and jerked it open. Dawn's white T-shirt was soaked with blood. In her arms, barely conscious, lay Sam. I cried: "What happened?"

Half-crying, half-frantic, Dawn said he had fallen off the play set and hit the back of his head: "Tim, do something!"

"Lay him down on the floor," I said, needing a second to think. Having Dawn hovering in such a state didn't help: "Run upstairs and grab me a face towel and a beach towel."

I looked at the back of Sam's head and found a crooked gash. I pulled off my own T-shirt and applied pressure. As Dawn bounded up the stairs, Sam moaned and whimpered. I checked his pupils, found they were reacting to light. I asked him, "What's your name?"

He responded slowly, "SSSaammmmm." The blood continued to ooze through my T-Shirt and onto the floor.

"What day is it?"

"Dooonn knooowwww," he slurred. I kicked myself for asking such a stupid question — even I didn't know what day it was. Dawn arrived back, frantic with energy. "Dawn, change your clothes and bring around the Suburban, we have to get him to a hospital."

By now the other kids had gathered round. I told one of them to fetch a blanket and laid it over Sam. Neighbours had begun to arrive so I recruited two of them to help load our kids into the truck and assist in our departure. As we began the thirty-minute drive to the hospital, Dawn, considerably calmer, gave me the details.

Sam had been climbing and swinging on the play set with the other kids. He had climbed to the top and attempted to swing, Tarzan style, to the top wrung of the adjacent equipment. He managed to grab the bar but then over-rotated and lost his grip. This sent him tumbling, awkwardly and head-first, towards the ground. The back of his head hit the bottom bar. He had fallen about eight feet. Dawn said: "I looked over just as it happened. He'd called, 'Hey, Mom, watch this!' Then, when his hands broke loose... do you know what he said?"

Dawn was crying again. I shook my head no.

"He said, 'Mom help me.'"

After x-raying Sam and checking him thoroughly, the doctor told us he had incurred only a slight concussion and would be fine. He would stitch him up and away we would go.

Back at the condo, with seven more stitches in his head, Sam had made a miraculous recovery: "Come on, Dad, let's go swimming."

That was Sam, that was my boy: knock him down and he would bounce right back up. As a five-year-old, Sam feared nothing — which, of course, scared me half to death. At the Shushwaps, I remained constantly on guard, especially when the kids were near the water. Juli and Laura were both good swimmers and I knew that. With Alana and Sam, however, the rule was: "If you're in the water or on the pier, you must be wearing a life jacket."

One day I was watching the kids from our balcony when I saw Sam face a dilemma. His life preserver was in the boat. The boat was tied up to the pier and his three sisters were paddling in the water and calling him, "Come on, Sam . . . it's fun." Rather than come and get his mother or me to retrieve his life jacket, Sam used the tie-rope to pull the boat over, climb in, don his life preserver and then jump into the water off the back of the boat.

This was a dangerous practice, so I went down to the dock and called Sam out of the water. Sternly I told him, "Don't ever do that again, Sam. Come and get Dad or Mom to help. I don't want you on the pier or near the boat without a lifejacket on."

"Okay, Dad," he said with a forlorn look.

But a few days later, as from the balcony I watched the girls swim, I stared dumbfounded as Sam, minus his life jacket, strolled out onto the pier and pulled the motorboat over with the tie-line. As he did so, two power boats went by — one in front of the other, drowning out my shouted command:

"Sam, come here!"

The waves bounced and rocked our boat. Sam stood with one foot on the dock and the other on the boat. Then, as our boat rocked away, unable to maintain his position, Sam dropped into the water and disappeared from view. I crashed through the back door, descended the stairs three at a time and sprinted to where I had last seen him.

Sam was frantically dog paddling and screaming for help. Waves poured into his mouth and also pushed our boat towards him, threatening to jam him against the wooden pier. The surface of the dock, which used forty-five-gallon drums for flotation, lay about thirty inches above the water — too high for Sam to get a grip. I considered jumping in but realized I would probably get sandwiched up against the pier and might lose track of my son.

I got down on my knees and, clinging to the dock with my left hand, grabbed for Sam with my right. Sam was in the valley of a wave and I missed by half a foot. The boat banged away at my head and shoulder and pressed the left side of my chest into the edge of the pier. I bore down to resist the boat, knowing that if it overpowered me, the V-shaped hull would simultaneously squeeze and submerge my boy. I positioned my torso between our boat and the pier while the up-and-down motion of the boat tortured me, jamming hard against a series of three ribs. I screamed, "Jesus F. Christ!"

With that, Sam's head bobbed up into my hand. A swell held him at the same level for a moment and I gathered a large hand full of his hair. As the swell gave way to a valley, Sam cried out while spitting, gurgling and spewing. Not wanting to deflate my lungs any further, I sadistically muttered under my breath, *Good you little rat, I hope it hurts like hell.* Another swell held him weightless for a moment, but then it passed and Sam's complaining escalated again.

At last our motorboat began rocking away from the dock, easing the weight against me. This was my chance. I yarded Sam up in a single motion. Facing me, both his hands trying in vain to release my grip, he managed to get first one foot and then the other onto the dock. With one last yank he fell on top of me as I collapsed onto my back. Sam held his scalp with both hands and cried uncontrollably. The sun felt so intense in my face and I just closed my eyes and held him tight with both arms.

Back in the condo, wrapped in a beach towel, Sam sobbed until he fell asleep. As I told Dawn about the series of events, she stood listening with both hands to her mouth. When I had finished, she went to the couch where he slept, picked him up and sat back down with him in her arms, the tears rolling down her face. Frankly, I was not moved to tears. My chest complained on each breath; my body twitched and pinged from the excess adrenaline. I was absolutely furious: *Good thing he's asleep*, I thought, *or I'd be entering into a spirited verbal tirade aimed at his stupidity and lack of obedience.*

* * *

That summer, Juli and Laura both learned to water ski, much to the envy of their younger siblings. One afternoon, I borrowed an additional ski-rope and a set of junior skis from our neighbour. The idea was to pull both girls behind our boat at the same time. On the very first try, both Juli and Laura popped out of the water and began skiing together. They waved to the boat and then to each other while Sam and Alana marveled at the event and then demanded to try the same. I said, "Sure, but first you have to learn how to ski by yourselves."

Both Alana and Sam tried numerous times to water ski that summer, but eventually asked to be returned to the boat. I knew the following summer, with some added coordination and strength, both would be successful.

The glorious, golden summer days of swimming, tubing and water skiing followed one after the other. On many occasions, we would opt to eat dinner away from home. "Finz" is a trendy restaurant on the lake. Patrons can arrive by water and moor almost at the front door. With our boat tied up and the kids in tow, we commandeered a table for six on the sunny side of the patio. We ordered two cold beers and four cold Cokes as the kids played (and Levi snoozed) in the adjoining park. Dawn and I basked in the warmth and joy that all parents experience, watching their kids romp and play in the sun.

When the drinks arrived, I called the kids but could account only for the three girls. Then, looking down the pier, I could scarcely believe my eyes. Sam was using the tie-up ropes to pull the boat over to climb into it, no permission, and no life jacket. Seating himself behind the wheel, Sam began enjoying himself immensely, pretending to be the captain under full throttle: "Vroooooommm!" His intuition picked me up half way down the pier. He turned right around and looked at me, his eyes widening with increasing dismay. As I boarded the boat, his voice trembled: "Dad, you're not mad, are you?"

Both Dawn and I had long since agreed that physical punishment of our children was simply not appropriate. Discipline by removing privileges, pointing out mistakes and errors — that was the way to go to make them accountable and responsible. Barbara Collorosa's wonderful theories about parenting went overboard as, bending Sam over my knee, I administered corporal punishment for only the second time in his five years: *Whack, whack!*

"Tell me why I spanked you," I demanded. Sam was a mess, literally out of control — upset, hurt, embarrassed, knowing I had lost respect for him. He tried unsuccessfully, sobbing jerkily, to put his thoughts into words. Once we had finished our man-to-man talk, I sat him on the pier with his life jacket on and told him: "Sam, you can join us when you are ready."

The rest of the vacation, Sam came to Dawn or me to ask permission to go on the pier or to go swimming. Each time I would ensure his life jacket was on and fastened properly, then thank him for asking. Some experts would say, "Spanking only creates fear in the child." I thought: *Fine, Sam can be fearful . . . if he won't fear the water and its associated dangers, he can bloody well be fearful of me!*

* * *

The Shuswaps brought back these memories and more. Even so, after a while, the sun, the water, the barbecues and the long, lazy days combined to relax, centre and ground our family. One evening, about the third or fourth day, as we sat around the campfire sharing stories and anecdotes, I noticed Dawn laughing and really enjoying herself. She was the Dawn I had known ten years before, the girl I had fallen in love with and married. Afterwards, I commented on the lightness of her heart and told her how much I enjoyed seeing her happy again, if only for a while.

Even at the Shushwaps, I tend to rise early. Three or four days a week, I'll play a round of golf. I can play a round quickly, get off the course and arrive back home just about the time Dawn and the kids are making themselves breakfast. Those days when I don't play golf, I like to walk. The morning after Dawn's light heart was a walking morning. Down the road, I had seen a vacant cottage for sale — one with a beautiful vista. I planned to walk to it, sit on the patio, look out over the lake and enjoy the sunrise. Technically, I might have been trespassing — but the owner and the realtor allowed propective buyers to come in and look around.

As I hiked towards the property early that morning, I said aloud to Sam, to the Universe, to God, to Buddha, to Jesus, to anyone who would hear me: "I want a profound statement that my son Sam is living beyond the physical. That my son Sam has become a spirit, has passed over and gone to heaven . . . I want unmistakable proof."

Although I had already received lots of proof, I was really saying: "You haven't called in a while. Pick up the phone!"

I carried on, enjoying the sunrise, when a number of butterflies began fluttering around me — the old familiar brown butterflies with white basting running around near the outside of their wings. One flew so close to me it brushed my eyelash. I stopped to rub my eye, and when I looked up, they were everywhere. I couldn't get away from them. The more butterflies I saw, the more I smiled, and the more I smiled, the more butterflies appeared. I felt that Sam had dug into his bag of tricks, rustled up a swarm of butterflies and sent them to greet me. I laughed like a child as the butterflies darted around me. Then, as suddenly as they had come, they began to disperse. I resumed walking and the farther I traveled, the fewer the butterflies.

As I neared the cottage, the sun rose behind me, warming my shoulders. As I arrived at the property, out of the corner of one eye, I caught movement. I looked at the chairs on the front deck and saw one of them gently rocking. I stopped short in my tracks, stared at the chair and thought: *the owners are here and they just went inside to get a coffee or something.* No, *that doesn't seem right.* I looked around but could see no vehicle. I noticed the padlocks on all the outside doors: the property was secure. Another possibility occurred to me: *maybe a houseboat had spent the night moored out front of the property. The occupants had come ashore but, seeing me arrive, scurried off thinking that I was the owner.* I called: "Hello! Can anybody hear me? I'm here admiring the property."

No answer. Again I called: "My name's Tim Johnson. I noticed your cottage for sale. I'm just out for a walk and I'm having a look around. I hope you don't mind. Wherever you are, please identify yourself."

My intellect discounted my intuition. It dismissed both the moving chair and my feeling that somebody else was present as figments of my imagination. In retrospect, I think of a quotation from a book called *The Gift of Fear* by Gavin DeBecker: "Intuition is catapulted to another level entirely," he wrote, "a height at which it can accurately be called graceful, even miraculous. Intuition is the journey from A to Z without stopping at any other letter along the way. It is knowing without knowing why."

After checking around the property, however, I surrendered to my intellect yet again and accepted that there was nobody there but me. Eventually, I sat down in the white chair — the one that seemed most appropriate. I sat enjoying the mirror-like calm of the water and the beauty of the trees, and then out of nowhere came a squirrel. It appeared on a log in front of me, ate something it held in its two paws, then scurried off again. A gaggle of Canada geese came flying towards me, honking, not ten feet above the surface of the water. As they drew near, they veered and headed straight north, giving me a chance to count them: there were seven.

Then, out of the corner of one eye, I noticed movement. I turned and studied the chair beside me. It couldn't be . . . rocking? The experience made me tingle, but warmly — as if Dawn or one of my children had touched me on the shoulder. I stared at the chair in awe as now it rocked back and forth. Someone who wasn't there might say a gust of wind rocked the chair or, in the absence of wind, a breeze created by the passing geese. In fact, there was no wind. And the geese were far enough below me that their motion could never have moved that chair.

As I sat watching, the chair rocked slowly back and forth. Suddenly, I had a very, very strong feeling that I was in the presence of an energy . . . an energy that was Sam's. I opened my heart to enjoy the moment . . . and started to weep. I didn't weep for missing Sam, or for my own broken heart, but rather because a dear, dear friend had stopped in to say hello. Eventually, the chair stopped rocking, but I sat in the sun for a long time afterwards, savoring the experience.

For the rest of the day, I enjoyed a wonderful sensed of groundedness. I knew that whatever was happening to me and my family was right and proper — that there was some purpose to this, an unfolding taking place. It was difficult, it was challenging, and I could certainly reason my way out of it or find ways to escape the whole process. However, when I remained open and available to these symbols and happenings, I experienced a whole new sense of wonder and awe. For the next couple of days, instead of going to play golf, I travelled back to the vacant property — where invariably I found the chair rocking chair.

This was an extraordinary gift — but soon I would discover that it was meant for me and me alone. I told my daughter Juli about the rocking chair and she wanted to see it. The next morning, instead of walking the five-mile round trip, Juli and I drove to the cabin. I had psyched her up for a special experience and felt terribly let down when Sam failed to show or at least to rock the chair. Juli and I must have look liked a couple of lunatics, staring for half an hour at this unmoving chair. Yet the next day, when again I went alone, with an open heart and grounded in my feelings and emotions, I waited only a short time, sitting in the white chair, before the chair beside me began to rock.

It was like an old friend had tapped me on the shoulder. I found myself remembering the evening, a few years before, when Dawn and I had rented the movie *Memphis Belle*. From the opening scene of this Second World War movie, I felt glued to the television screen, fully in the moment. Each scene jarred loose a memory in me, together with feelings of tension, apprehension and, most of all, fear. In another lifetime, I had been there. The only difference between the movie and my own experience was that the crew of the Memphis Belle had returned home after twenty-five missions. I never made it.

I've already described how, whenever I'm *Being Clean*, information comes to me in a flash of intuition. I receive an insight about a person, an event that has happened or even one that will happen. Sometimes I receive a full-blown premonition, and other times I get a flash about an event that happened to me in the past, before this lifetime, in a kind of regression. One of my most vivid regressions, and one I've experienced half a dozen times in the past three or four years, starts with a series of brilliant flashes of white light, each lasting perhaps one ten-thousandth of a second, but carrying a hundred thousand bits of information.

I am in my late teens or early twenties. It is dark, just before sunrise, and I am riding a bicycle over a pot-holed, rain-drenched road. From time to time I raise my legs as I splash through a puddle. I am on my way to breakfast. I am a bomber pilot during the Second World War. I am badly hung over as I drink myself into a stupor after each mission, just as I will again tonight, if I return....

My last flash of this particular regression came about one month before Sam's passing, while he and I were quietly playing on the floor of our cottage. During this flash, my plane has been hit and has started its death spin. That's when the aircraft begins to rotate in a spiral while plunging towards earth. It is a death spin because the ever-increasing "G" forces pin the occupants to the wall of the aircraft. Crew members can not jump out; they can not move; they are as if cemented in place, very much alive and very much aware as they rapidly approach the ground.

As the death spin pastes me to the wall, I struggle in vain to escape the plane. Soon the "G" forces are so great that I can not even move. I can only think. In that final moment, I look across the aircraft into the eyes of one of my crew . . . my younger brother. As our eyes meet, we communicate our mutual understanding without uttering a word: we both know that we are about to die. As the motors scream, pulling us into a tighter and tighter spiral, my heart breaks and I begin weeping for my brother.

At this point, I am yanked out of my regression and back into our cottage in Millarville by something Sam says evenly and deliberately and completely out of the blue: "You remember the airplane, don't you?"

Flabbergasted, almost speechless, I stare goggle-eyed at Sam and splutter: "What . . . what did you just say?"

Sam looks back at me, his manner calm and matter of fact: "You're not really my father, you know." He speaks clearly and lucidly. "You're my brother."

And with that, he resumes playing.

I sit there totally dumbfounded. Finally, feeling the weight of every word, I ask again: "Sam . . . what do you mean?"

But he won't answer. He just keeps playing.

No matter. I am so filled with magic and energy that I want this moment to last forever. Several times after that, and right up until the day of his passing, Sam looked up at me and said: "You're the best Dad I ever had . . . but, really, we are brothers, you know."

CHAPTER TWENTY-ONE

CONNECTING WITH SAM

Settling into our Millarville home after ten days in "summer paradise" proved difficult. Where before we had spent hot, blissful days waterskiing, tubing or cruising around the lake, now we sought escape from the sweltering dry heat in an overcrowded outdoor swimming pool. Once the pool closed for the day, we would stand in line for ice cream behind chain-smoking, multi-pierced Canadian teenagers, bobbing to American rap music. Moments after leaving the pool, and even after a refreshing shower, we would all be miserable again because it took the air conditioner ten minutes to turn the leather-clad interior of the Suburban from a raging inferno merely to frying-pan hot.

Once home, we would take refuge in the cool basement of the new house, which was still under construction. Juli was the first to speak up: "Dad, this really sucks. Can't we go back to the lake, please?" Laura and Alana, elated that Juli had given voice to their sentiments exactly — and also at the thought of returning to paradise — enthusiastically seconded this motion: "Yeah, Dad! Let's go right now."

Knowing this was not possible, and brimming with enthusiasm, I did my best Roberto Benigni imitation, complete with Italian accent, pointing out the highlights of spending July and August on our farm. "We can sleep in here tonight, nice and cool and have a pajama party. I'll rent a movie and bring in TV. We can cook bacon and beans on new fireplace. Tomorrow we take each towels down to pond, and when hot, we run and jump in and swim to dock. What you say to that, my little bambinos?"

Dejectedly, Juli said, "Dad, this is just not as much fun as the lake."

I had to agree. This wasn't much fun — but would the lake have been much better? The problem wasn't our environment, it was us. Sam was always such a spark plug — especially at the lake in the summer. Swimming, laughing, joking — it was like he was constantly auditioning for the role of "village idiot." We missed him so much, not just his energy, but the way he acted as the catalyst for fun. In a word, we all felt . . . miserable.

I kept asking myself why this summer, of all summers? Why, after all this family had been through, why wouldn't the universe give us some healing time at the lake? That night, as Dawn and I got ready for bed, she asked what was bothering me. I opened up and shared my frustration. When I was finished, I said: "So there it is."

Dawn said: "Tim, I know you and the kids were really enjoying the lake. But all the time we were there, I just wanted to be at home."

If Dawn wanted to be at home, fair enough: I was fine with that. Not another word of complaint would pass my lips. I didn't imagine, then, that there might be a reason why we'd come home. The days dragged on and a fleeting happiness came and went. At times, I was glad to be home — at least the surroundings were familiar. I would get up early each morning and walk down to the pond. Just sitting there, taking in the visual beauty and pleasant sounds of that place, helped ground and nurture me. The sweltering hot days kept coming and we did our best to enjoy them.

One day, the phone rang...a call we would never have received if we had remained in the Shushwaps. Janet, an old family friend, was telephoning from Toronto to say we'd been on her mind for the past week and she just had to connect. She didn't know why, but she felt a need to mention that she had a friend who was a medium, who could communicate with passed-over spirits. She wondered, hesitantly, if we had ever considered trying to connect with Sam's spirit through someone like her friend.

Just a few weeks previous, another friend had given us a book called *The Eagle and the Rose* by Rosemary Altea. It's about a woman who discovers that she has a gift — that she can connect with spirits. The book had intrigued me so much that I had drafted a letter to request a "sitting," and I had planned to mail it the same day Janet called. About this, I said nothing. I knew Dawn well enough to wait until she volunteered her feelings about attempting any such communication. That evening in bed, she brought it up: "Tim, I have so many unanswered questions. I feel I would like to contact Janet's friend and see what she has to say."

The following day, Dawn arrived in the Quonset hut and announced: "I just spoke with Frannie, the woman Janet told us about. You know, the medium...the person who may be able to help us connect with Sam's spirit."

Dawn had arranged to call Frannie again in a few days, at eleven o'clock in the morning, when perhaps she would have something for us. My heart leapt. I anticipated that Sam would walk into that medium's home. Dawn and I would ask questions and Sam would respond through her. It would be a dialogue with Frannie acting as translator. I sat down and wrote out twelve questions. Come the appointed day, I entered my office promptly at ten forty-five. I centred the speaker phone on the table and set out a chair for Dawn. I felt beside myself with excitement. Was this going to be my chance to connect with my son? My chance to have some closure with him . . . to tell him I loved and missed him?

Dawn arrived to find me fidgety and wide-eyed: "What's with you?"

"Oh, Dawn. I really want this to work."

When Dawn is centred, as she was at this moment, she is at her best. "Tim, you are far too attached to the outcome of this experience," she said slowly. "Take some deep breaths and relax. This woman may have nothing for us. Let's just take this one step at a time."

Dawn's words calmed me. As she dialed the phone, I took several deep breaths and began to feel better. After some polite introductory conversation, Frannie asked if we had time to continue. Dawn said, "Yes, we have a neighbor sitting with the children — go ahead, Frannie."

Frannie said she was staying with her sister at a cottage on a lake north of Toronto. She had not been feeling well because her sister had painted a room and the fumes had affected her. Yet she had managed to do some work and today she felt much better. Dawn asked how she had discovered her gift. Frannie said she had been working as a model. At photo shoots, spirits would often approach her and give her information to pass on. She found making these connections, and surprising stupefied friends and family, immensely gratifying: she had found her calling.

Frannie asked if we wished to continue? I felt she was really asking: "Do you think I'm for real? Do we have chemistry? Do you want to work with me?"

Dawn glanced over at me at I nodded my approval. She said: "Yes, we would like to go ahead."

Frannie spent a few minutes describing what she

had received since speaking originally with Dawn. She had made notes and now read them to us. She described an instance of "lucid dreaming" in which she had seen someone holding "a goose or a duck, maybe a swan." At one point she saw an adult male walking. It was like watching a film and she zoomed in on the man's arm: "Right arm going to grab a child's hand — no child." After that, she awoke with a feeling of tightness in her chest.

Later, after meditating, she had connected telepathically with Dawn. She watched as, while Dawn lay sleeping, Sam visited her. Frannie saw him arrive and enter her dream state. As she did so, Frannie thought: "Dawn may remember. I hold the space for her to remember the visit."

The following day, Frannie again saw Sam, only this time he was curiously looking through her bedroom window, leaning against it, his hands cupped around his eyes so he could see inside. And then he was with her, in her presence. Upon further meditation, Frannie described what she experienced, speaking into a tape recorder: "Samuel came into my space and spoke to me for a very long time. It was like talking to a dear friend. There were sounds of Canada geese out on the lake honking as I was in purple light and the gentle energy of his beautiful presence. He took me to the dock on the pond and I was a part of the energy of it all, so that I could experience what this place was. He kept speaking gently as I asked questions. I wanted to write but he said it was important for me to experience this communication. Then my sister Colleen came into the room and I spoke from this expanded state and asked her to listen to the words and she turned on the tape recorder. Samuel's energy moved with mine. I felt a oneness so that I could bring through his thoughts of information. When our communication ended, the Canada geese flew away honking as I felt

Samuel's energy leave — or maybe I should say, I left his energy. I know why I had to come to the lake house now — to witness the Canada geese and how Sam is using them to form his energy and bring communication to our hearts."

The following day, Frannie awoke early, drifted into a meditative state and again felt Sam's presence. He invited her to join him outside on the dock, said he had something to show her. She kept seeing a dog, black and white, and also birds flying. She heard geese squawking and an orchestral rendition of *Old McDonald Had A Farm*. All of nature had become a glorious symphony. Soon afterwards, she received these words:

Dear Mom and Dad,
    This is a letter to you as I am still connected so to your life. Your thoughts and prayers help me because it is an energy. As human beings we are living on the earth fulfilling only part of the whole that exists. When you are conscious of other dimensional selves then you can expand your awareness. As a six-year-old boy I lived the part of me that could remember the soul. Now as spirit, I am living energy able to connect with presence to all other dimensions. As you, my soul continues to evolve the same as all yet now there is no fear.
    This does not exist as energy in a place as I am. There are schools here too in a different way. There is not the time as you know it but there are moments of understanding that there are certain structures pertaining to levels of conscious awareness. As all of the ones we perceive as leaving each dimension can choose to re-enter into other body or move into higher learning in realm beyond the physical. Many choose to be in body to help other souls reach

the awareness of other dimensions in body. This is all for each individual soul and the contracts of group souls.

My life span in a body was to be of a few years and if the ones choosing to be with one in body would have awakened in a more conscious way then it was my choice to stay or not. The choice was made to leave at this time for the growth of the masses, not just for our immediate family. There will be much more expressed to you about this matter. The understanding of the death will help many. The continuation of my own understanding will help you. There are no doubts in the mind of the heart. The heart chooses to not blame anyone especially your selves. The fear that is developed from the thoughts of unlovingness is the greatest tragedy of all.

There may be a celebration in hearts when the human kind understands the perfection of all events in life and the release of pain and suffering need not be a life long experience. The struggles around death are only created by the mind that does not believe in the truth of living spirit. God is the experience that Heaven is. It's all Heaven even on earth if one chooses to live present in the heart. The expression of Hell is a place where humans put themselves because they cannot face the thought of being in total oneness with God, losing their own ego description of self.

There are many opportunities for you now to remember the gifts of our moments together in earthly bodies and know that it is all energy living on in everything you will ever know. Forgive yourselves for the moments you forgot that you were Heaven and let yourself be this space for many souls who are searching for the moment of remembering. There are only "one" and together the truth will free all to be creating what I am in Spirit.

Sam in Spirit

I love you

Frannie addressed a brief note to Dawn and me, saying she realized what Sam had been doing: "He was showing me Heaven on Earth through his eyes. He was also showing me how multi-dimensional we are. Maybe children have a feeling of it more easily because they can be more present and in imagination. I have sat on the dock many times through my growing up. I have never experienced Nature serenade me so loudly and all at once. He was definitely getting my attention to focus fully so that the letter could come through. Now when the letter is finished nature shares her beauty but it's softer and more spacious. A beautiful morning to know God . . . ."

As Frannie finished, I felt light, calm and at peace. Softly, from a distance, Frannie said: "How are you doing, Dawn? Tim?" Dawn was quite emotional and, if she had spoken, she would have done so through tears. I said, "Frannie, this has been a very special moment for us. We will say goodbye now and check in with you later."

Gently, we all three signed off.

I took a pillow from the couch and lay down on the floor, my mind quiet, my heart open. As tears rolled down my face, I felt I was glimpsing the divine beauty of my experience of Sam's passing. . . .

CHAPTER TWENTY-TWO

A SENSE OF DESTINY

The session with Frannie taught me a new appreciation for symbolic communication. Looking at the list of questions I had prepared before that long-distance conversation, I felt slightly ridiculous. I had wanted to ask Sam what he was thinking when he walked down that road. Why did he walk out onto the ice? Also things like: who met him on the other side after he passed over? Had he left behind unfinished business? Where exactly was he?

Once again, I was intellectualizing. It was like I was saying, "How was your trip? Is the food okay?" Frannie's communication was more symbolic than I had anticipated, more imagistic — more like what I had already been receiving. Sam on the dock at the lake in the sunshine, and the geese, the frogs, the crickets and more playing out like a symphony. I began to understand that Sam and the spirit world were continuously present, and as long as I remained open and clear, the symbols would come. My questions had simply been the wrong ones. Through Frannie, Sam had communicated: "Stop asking and listen!"

The symbolic communication was as if someone I loved had begun speaking Latin or a language that I did not know. At first I might try to pick up on gestures and inflections but these could take me only so far. The best solution would be for me to learn Latin. If I chose not to do so, I would never fully understand what my loved one was seeking to communicate. Such was the situation I faced with Sam. Frannie had zeroed in not only on the black and white dog (Patches), but on images and symbols that I, too, had been picking up, like the Canada geese.

She also alluded to things I had mentioned to nobody — a feeling of tightness in my chest, for example. Whenever I feel stressed or emotionally tense, I tend to hold my pent-up emotions and energy in my chest. Since April 7, I had been trying to contain an absolute ocean of emotion. Often my chest felt extremely tight . . . so tight that I found it difficult to breathe. It was like I was constantly waiting to exhale but was unable to do so.

Above all, I identified with Frannie's image of the man walking. When Sam was alive, he and I would often walk hand in hand. Since his passing, I have had numerous dreams in which I reach for him, unable to touch him, unable to pull him from the water. When I awake my right shoulder aches. It's a dull, non-stop ache that never really goes away, not even to this day.

I began to understand that my intuition provides subtle information, never a drum roll or a trumpet blast, but something far more delicate, something faint and simple yet extremely profound. When Frannie described how sensitive she was to paint fumes, I understood. A medium would almost have to be extremely impressionable. Had Frannie connected with Sam's spirit or energy? In my view, yes, absolutely….

Even so, I felt terribly let-down — like a child who receives birthday gifts he has already seen. The medium had delivered no eurekas, no surprises, only confirmations. My disappointment stemmed from having wanted someone else to do the work for me — to bring me profound information about my son or my son's spirit. I was let down because of my own expectations. Realizing that, I caught a glimpse of the real task at hand. My journey was not to be led by a shaman, a priest, a rabbi, a minister, a gifted medium or anyone else. It was to be led by me. If I wanted a more intimate, more profound relationship with my son, I would have to go deeper. I would have to work harder on myself, trusting and following the guidance of my own intuition....

That evening, on a whim, I rented a family movie called *Simon Birch*. Based on a remarkable novel by John Irving, perhaps best-known for *The World According to Garp*, it's a tender work with a powerful spiritual message. The title character is both a strange young boy and a child of destiny — someone who is fated from the start to die early while laying down his life for others. With the Johnson family, *Simon Birch* really hit home. By the end of the movie, the girls were openly weeping, the tears flowing freely down their cheeks. I marveled at how easily the hurt flowed out of them, at how open their hearts were, and envied them for having something I had forgotten, or perhaps needed to remember.

Some people will think I'm crazy, but I believe that, in some way, Sam was meant to leave us when he did; that his passing was part of a larger plan involving fate or karma — what Hindus and Buddhists call the dharma. That's what *Simon Birch* brought home. The little boy in that film was predestined to be taken early and I feel the same is true of Sam.

Every time I read Sam's channelled message, I gain new insights. *The choice was made to leave at this time for the growth of the masses, not just for our immediate family. There will be much more expressed to you about this matter. The understanding of the death will help many.* As time rolls by, Sam's passing becomes less and less a puzzlement to me and more of a challenge of epic proportions. His passing is the ultimate lure for me to challenge myself, go deeper and continue to evolve and my creator knows this. My creator knows I will never stop looking for my son . . . that I will search for Sam until I find him.

* * *

My grieving seems to run in cycles. Sometimes I am still so angry I feel consumed by it. But other times I work through the grief and begin to pick up on the real message or messages. Perhaps sharing Sam's story will reveal another piece of the puzzle. Will someone come to me with more information? Will my experience perhaps stimulate others to pursue their own unanswered questions? For me, searching for Sam has become a lifelong spiritual quest.

The movie *Simon Birch* also reminded me of my recurring premonition — of the message I received repeatedly over the years that something devastating was going to happen when I was around age forty. That, even more specifically, I was going to suffer the loss of someone very dear to me. Also, I remembered the way I felt on April 7, the day of the fateful event — my feeling in the morning that we should not leave, which I articulated to Dawn. And then my bizarre restlessness, my out-of-character behaviour: despite my best efforts to shake it off, a sense of forboding ate away at me all day.

Finally, I looked at the flawlessness of "the plan's" execution. Dawn and I had been taken off site. If Sam had fallen through the ice when I was present, I would never have stopped trying to reach him and would probably died trying. If Sam were meant still to be here, he would have snagged his coat when he jumped off the dock, and so dangled with his head above water until rescuers could reach him. Or maybe the ice would have held him. Or Barbara or

Juli Ann would have spotted him hiding on their first pass in the truck. Or Robert would have been able to make his way across the ice and, while standing on the dock, scooped him out of the icy water. Or else Sam would not have lost consciousness before drowning: his mammalian reflex would have kicked in and kept his lungs free of water, in which case the doctors could probably have revived him.

However, the harsh reality remains: none of these things occurred. Instead, Sam was taken from us. Did this happen without reason? Was his passing without meaning? Only if God or some karmic, spiritual, universal reality doesn't exist. And that I couldn't and can't believe.

After *Simon Birch,* as the girls got ready for bed, I noticed how sad they felt. Obviously, the movie had touched the grief they felt at the loss of their brother. They were going deeper. We told no stories that night, did no chatting. The girls remained reflective, safe in their own spaces....

A sense of destiny, then. I resolved to remain more open to the universe, to become still more sensitive to whatever it was communicating. Two events now confirmed me in this approach. The first arrived second-hand — more an affirmative echo than anything else. Dawn happened to have a candid conversation with a woman from Millarville. This woman, named Carol, had no children of her own, but her brother and sister-in-law had died in a car crash and she had become the legal guardian of their two daughters. During the first year and a half of her guardianship, she constantly wondered whether she had made the right decision for the girls and herself.

Then one day a stranger knocked on her door — a middle-aged, native North American woman who asked if her name was Carol. Answered affirmatively, the visitor said: "I have a message for you. I was wondering if I can come in and tell it to you."

Carol did not know this woman but felt her sincerity and invited her into the house. They sat and visited for a while and finally Carol said, "What is this message? What have you come to tell me?"

The woman told her that, two days before, she had been participating in a sweat lodge. She explained that this is like entering a sauna in which the heat and steam are very intense. Once she let herself go, she entered a vision state in which spirits came and spoke with her. One of them had identified Carol as his sister and asked this woman to deliver a message. Remembering her dead brother, Carol felt a chill go down her spine. The woman continued: "The message is that your brother wants you to know that you have made the right choice, and he thanks you for it, and he's around you and the girls all the time."

After delivering this message, the visitor excused herself and left, never to be heard from again. Carol drew sustenance from this experience — and so did some of those who heard about it, like Dawn and me.

The second event, more personally focused, involved one of Sam's friends, Taylor Weinberger, son of Jode and Dwight. He is an active, energetic, rambunctious boy who loves wrestling, running, trampolining or playing Batman and Robin. More than once, I imagined Taylor and Sam as teenagers, perhaps running a summertime landscaping business. Looking at the two of them, I would think about pick-up trucks. Sometimes I would see them as eighteen or nineteen years old — virile young men wearing blue jeans and T-shirts who, at the end of a long day, would end up sitting on the tailgate of their pick-up truck, drinking cold beer, belching and talking about girls.

For Taylor's fifth birthday, Sam picked out a gift at the Millarville general store, insisting adamantly that Taylor would like it. It was a bubblegum tape machine, which looks like a regular scotch tape dispenser but is filled with a tape of bubble gum. The user tears off a one-inch, two-inch, three-inch or even a horkin' six-inch piece of bubble gum and pockets the machine for later. Of all the things that Taylor received that birthday, he still remembers that bubble gum tape machine.

Dawn and Taylor's mother, Jode, visit back and forth regularly. A couple of days after the session with Frannie, Jode told Dawn she had a story to share. While walking to the Millarville General Store, Jode had offered to buy Taylor one treat. The boy said, "I want a bubble gum tape machine like the one Sam gave me for my birthday."

Jode agreed to buy that. At the store, as they approached the bubble gum tape rack, suddenly it fell apart: to their surprise, all of the bubble gum tape dispensers spilled out onto the floor in front of them. Taylor exclaimed: "Mom! it just . . . it just, like, exploded . . . why did it do that?"

Jode felt somewhat embarrassed, thinking that those in the store would suspect that either she or Taylor had knocked the display to the ground. As they stood amazed among the strewn bubble gum tape machines, in unison they said, "It must be Sam!"

The story hit home with Dawn. Shortly after Jode left, Dawn sat down on the couch and said out loud, "Sam . . . I love these stories, I really do love hearing them, but I want proof. I want something to prove to me that you exist out there beyond the physical, and that you can communicate with me. Sam, I want something."

Dawn wept for a while and then went about her routine. She decided to collect the recyclables and run them into town when the children arrived home from school. As she gathered and separated items on the porch, she spotted some shiny tin cans lying out behind the house. Probably the cats, finding traces of food, had carted them back there for a private snack. After picking them up, Dawn turned to go back to the house and stopped in her tracks. Immediately before her lay Sam's last-purchased bubble gum tape machine, opened, but barely used....

CHAPTER TWENTY-THREE

PRESENT IN THE HEART

Having communicated with Sam symbolically, I drew up a checklist of conditions that make such communication possible. (This organizing would appear to come from my intellect, wanting now to co-operate with my emotions.) I had learned that, while opening myself up, I must disconnect with any negativity that exists in my life. I must quiet the chattering monkeys (the battle between intellect and emotion) and then focus, putting awareness on my awareness. I must allow my consciousness to drop into my heart and remain there with my openness. Finally, I must allow myself to exist in the moment between thoughts . . . to *Be Clean*.

Since Sam has passed, I have made other observations. If I drink alcohol, for example, even just a little, I cannot connect, cannot *Be Clean*. Alcohol prevents me from being present in the moment between thoughts, and so prevents any possible connection or experience. Alcohol is a refuge, a place for me to hide — though it doesn't work for me and I now choose to abstain. I don't use mind-altering drugs either, but I suspect that if I did, they too would take me out of the deeper experiences.

Another situation that will stop me from *Being Clean* is if I'm upset, either at myself or with somebody else. When I do get upset, I need to express the negative energy through cathartic pillow-pounding, wood chipping, yelling or screaming. As I become more aware, I incorporate more activities that allow me to be centred, and I rid myself of those involvements that don't. The more "clean" and grounded I become, the more guiding information I receive and the less need I feel for alcohol, sugar, TV or other stimulations, the closer I move to my family and friends . . . the closer I move to my creator.

In the days that followed our session with Frannie, I realized that the way in which Sam as a spirit showed himself to me was the same way he manifested to Frannie — through dreams and symbols in nature. I knew Frannie was tapping into Sam's spirit because the information she relayed strongly resemble that which I had received. My feeling was that Sam was guiding me or directing me with these experiences. My feeling has always been that my life on earth is about evolving and improving myself, about courageously moving forward.

Another realization, still more powerful, emerged out of the message from Sam that Frannie had channeled: *There may be a celebration in hearts when the human kind understands the perfection of all events in life and the release of pain and suffering need not be a life long experience . . . . It's all heaven even on earth if one chooses to live present in the heart.*

I realized that Dawn had set a beautiful, courageous example for me and the children. From the instant we received news of Sam's passing, she had jumped right into the "grief end of the pool" without reservation. She remained so fully "present in the heart." I, on the other hand, had taken an elevator approach to grieving. I would get in, push the button and descend one floor. The doors would open up and the grief that confronted me, challenging me to go places I had never gone before, frightened me so much that frantically I would push the "close door" button. Back at ground level, my intellect would rescue my emotion and say: "We will go back there another time, no need to deal with that today. You have to look after Dawn and the kids."

I knew that I had infinite levels of grief to explore. Also, I yearned for a more intimate relationship with my heart — a more open heart so I could have a closer bond with my family, my friends and my son's spirit. One evening, sitting at my desk in the Quonset hut, I picked up a pen and paper and began writing . . .

> Sometimes I get angry…. Angry at Sam for his stupidity, for his lack of reason, respect or reverence. Angry for his inability to listen, to mind, to heed our warnings, to obey…. Angry at him for leaving me alone, lonely and devastated….
>
> Sometimes I am embarrassed and ashamed…. embarrassed for not being there that fateful day, embarrassed that I had lost such a prized part of me and my life. Ashamed that I didn't save him or, at the very least, die trying….
>
> Sometimes the memory of my son Sam is so distant…it seems as if he was only a figment of my imagination, someone who never really existed….
>
> Sometimes, in the morning when I wake up, my body feels like it's made out of lead…. It takes all my strength to lift myself up and go about the days toil….
>
> Sometimes I am teetering on an edge, hanging on by my fingernails…. I hope no one will bring up his name, no one will mope or cry or be sad. Because the slightest hint of emotion will send me tumbling into despair, and I don't want to go there…maybe tomorrow but please, not today….

Sometimes I bargain with my Lord.... Bargain with him to take me back to the moment before Sam walked out on the ice. Bargain with him to take me now so I no longer have to deal with the pain of the loss....

Sometimes I'm glad it is cloudy and rainy.... It's as if the sky is echoing my feelings. Gloomy, sad and listless....

Sometimes I will run into a friend and we will laugh and kibbitz and I will feel good.... Then later I will be alone and sad and feel guilty for the happy moments I had....

Sometimes I think of how Sam threw himself headlong into his life.... With all the passion and enthusiasm he could muster, and how beautiful he was in doing so....

Sometimes I have a dream about Sam.... It is so vivid that I awake and search the house for him in vain....

Sometimes I think about when Sam came into our room in the middle of the night after he had a bad dream.... How I would comfort him, and hold him, and tell him he could sleep with us and promise to stay awake until he fell asleep....

Sometimes I sit and think of him ...and then the phone rings and I don't know what day it is, I don't know what time it is, and I unplug the phone because the ringing tears at me....

Sometimes when Dawn is late coming home and I can't reach her on the car phone.... I expect the RCMP to arrive with tragic news....

Sometimes I see Sam's young friends at the general store...healthy and laughing and having a Coke, and I am so crushed that I run out the back door before I completely fall apart....

Sometimes I feel a dull ache...in the bottom of my stomach that stays all day.... Sometimes

I get a red hot spark of memory.... And I am instantly back in the moments immediately after Sam's death. Charged with all the emotion, grief, shock and dismay....

Sometimes I look at my son Levi's face and think I'm looking at Sam.... Sometimes I see something in nature and know it is moved by his energy and spirit. And sometimes I can sense the beauty and wonder and grace and flawless order of the universe, and know he is safe and protected and totally "ok".

Sometimes I know Sam was one hundred per cent obedient...one hundred per cent obedient to his zest for life, one hundred per cent obedient to his thirst and curiosity, one hundred per cent obedient to his own guardian angel who told him to kiss his mother and father goodbye and come follow me....

But always...I miss my son....

When I read this over, I realized that I needed to give myself a chance fully to explore the depths of my grief. I wondered if maybe I should go through the Hoffman Process again? The more I pondered it, the more it really seemed to fit — time to deal with my issues in a safe environment. Dawn approved the idea and, late in July, I left her and the kids for a nine-day retreat during which I would re-experience the Hoffman Process.

During the first two days, I again dealt with the negative aspects of my parents — tendencies to withdraw, to seek escape in alcohol, addictions, the list went on. Then came defence work: "Why they did what they did." My sense was, I wasn't just repeating the Process, but finding new, unaddressed issues or issues that were layered...I was going deeper.

Four days into the process, having expressed

most of the negative energy arising out of my relations with my parents, and with the "chattering monkeys" quieted, I felt clear and quiet. I possessed a solitude I hadn't felt since before Sam's passing. I was centred, grounded and "present in my heart." At that point, a childhood memory flashed into my consciousness with all the vivid color and detail of the original experience.

My hysterical mother ran through the house to the phone. She screamed something into the receiver. Moments later, firemen broke down my parent's bedroom door. Thick black smoke filled our home as someone carried me out onto the front lawn and wrapped me in an itchy wool blanket. Moments later, the biggest fireman in the world walked out of our house and down the stairs carrying my little sister Laureen in his arms.

That day marked many things in my young life. It marked the last day I would ever see my little sister alive. It marked the day my Mom would begin to overcompensate for everyone and everything. It marked the day that my father would permanently withdraw into either his work or alcohol.

Beginning to understand, for the first time, why my parents had behaved the way they did sent me spinning. That evening I was afforded quiet time. Still in a highly reflective state, I retreated to my room. There, as I lay on the bed with a clean and open heart, my childhood experiences hammered away at me. Through adult eyes, I was witnessing my mother and father acting out their dysfunctional behaviour around the untimely death of their daughter Laureen. Experience after experience rolled over me like tidal waves, one after another.

Finally, I was glimpsing the world through my parents' eyes. My heart opened up to them — not with pity, not with shame, but with my deepest compassion. Sobbing, moaning and finally wretching, I descended to levels within myself I had never dreamed existed. Deeper and deeper I sank, feeling the hurt and loss and grief of a lifetime. From the deepest part of my soul, the emotion worked its way out of my body, out of my pores, out of my eyes, out of my throat.... The next morning, my teacher asked me how I was feeling. The tears flowed freely down my cheeks, but my voice remained steady and clear: "Better."

Still, the next two days proved a roller-coaster of emotion. One moment down, feeling the depth of my emotion, the next moment up, feeling light and energized. Then came closure — the making of a final peace with mother and father. I remembered most of the Hoffman Process from my first time through, but this part I had forgotten.

The week had been emotionally draining. As the teachers brought it to a close, my mind raced ahead to reuniting with Dawn and the kids and enjoying the balance of the summer with them before school started. Then my teacher said something that yanked me back into the room: "With your eyes still closed, see any children that have pre-deceased you to your right." In my mind's eye, there was Sam sitting quietly, calmly, with an impish grin that said, "Hey, Dad! How ya doin'?"

The teacher went on, "Take this time to clear any issues you may have with them so that you may have closure." It was like someone had pushed me over Niagara Falls. I fell further and further and further down and broke completely apart. The compassionate, emotional depths of feeling I had reached two days before, while dealing with my parents, stood revealed as shallows along a rocky shore as now I plunged into a dark abyss. There was nothing to stop or even slow my descent. For the first time in relation to the passing of my son, Samuel Jess Johnnson, I was "fully present in my heart" and experiencing the awesome depth of grief and despair that were mine...

CHAPTER TWENTY-FOUR

LIVING IN THE MOMENT

So there it was: my life's work laid out before me. Was I willing to go through, not around, these most difficult experiences to arrive at a better place? Was I willing to be humble, open, afraid and vulnerable? Was I willing to do my work? Willing to lead rather than be led? Willing to evolve? Was I willing to make the transformation from caterpillar to butterfly?

Had I finally, during the Hoffman Process, dealt with the pent-up emotions left by the death of my son? No, not hardly. I think that finally I had started to deal with those emotions. Finally I had stopped walking through my life on eggshells, hoping nothing else bad would ever happen to me again. Finally, I had started to live and breathe again....

My first night home after my retreat, I had the following dream:

I am in the den of our new home when a vision appears as a hologram in the middle of the room, as if projected from somewhere else — the kind of thing that happened in Star Wars with R2D2. The image is of an immaculately dressed man in a pin-stripe suit, crisp white shirt with round gold buttons and black patent shoes with a mirror finish. He wears his hair in a ponytail and sports a neatly trimmed goatee. He asks: "Are you feeling pain, my friend?"

I say nothing but think my response: "Yes."

He picks this up clearly, registers all the emotion, perceives every nuance, and nods his understanding: "Is your pain caused by the loss of your son?"

Again, as I think, "Yes," he reads the message beneath the message, picks up the tightness in my chest, my apprehension, my fear. His amazing perceptiveness concerns me and I realize that I must be extremely careful of what I think.

The man says, "No my friend. You don't."

I put my feelings on guard and clear my mind. Now I feel safe. The man says nothing. He seems confused by the calm openness of my mind and immediately makes his proposition: "If given free will and choice, would you like to travel back in time to ease your pain? Back to the last day you spent with your son when he was still alive?"

As the word "alive" leaves his lips, I am magically transported back in time to observe from a distance parts of my last day with Sam. But the vision is fast, incomplete and lacking in detail, and I am quickly returned to the den.

My heart is pounding. I yearn to be returned to the vision of Sam. This must be what a lifetime heroin addict feels, these pangs of withdrawal, because I know I would sell my soul and everyone dear to me for another moment back in that time.

I'm still spinning emotionally, so the well-dressed man holds my hand and grounds me by saying: "It's okay, my friend. I am here for you. My heart goes out to you. But please let me show you another possibility."

Again, I am magically transported, this time to the cold woods in the foothills of the Rockies near where I live. I am kneeling, crying uncontrollably, yearning for my son so much I want to end my pathetic life, my only solace being that, on the other side, Sam will greet me. At the same time I know I will not spend much time with him, that I will go elsewhere to pay my karmic debt and be assigned other work and lessons. I know that I will be with him only for a moment, yet that is so tempting I want to pull the trigger of the gun that rests in my lap.

As I cock the hammer and point the gun I am instantly back in the den again, holding the hand of the well-dressed man as he stokes my head with his free hand: "My friend, it's okay. Let me comfort you."

My torment is immense. In the blink of an eye, suddenly I am reduced to being barbecued alive on a spit over hot coals, the skewer forced in through my anus and out my left shoulder, narrowly missing all of my vital organs, and ensuring my prolonged torture as I'm turned over and over.

"Now my son — you must choose."

Tremendous energy is pulling me in two opposing directions at once.

My shoulders ache, my head pounds, and I realize that whatever I choose will rip me from my anus through my shoulders, separating my head and my heart for all eternity, and leaving me here in purgatory, roasting on this spit forever.

Waiting, the well-dressed man hisses, delighting in my dilemma in a perverse sexual way. I gather all my strength and pull myself together from the inside, and in a moment of clarity, my wordless answer springs forth from within: "I choose to reside here, in the moment between the thoughts."

With that, a high-pitched, metallic snap echoes through my mind. My arms go limp and the unbearable traction on my body is released. At the same time, instantly, the hologram vanishes and I am filled with a peace around the passing of my son that I had never before experienced.

I awake into reality, throw on my clothes and walk to the pond. I remove my shoes, sit on the dock and dangle my feet in the water. The light breeze smells of ozone and refreshes me. The golden sunrise warms my back and lights up the landscape. Geese circle the pond, honking to communicate their chosen landing area. Fixing their wings with rigid landing gear, they turn from fliers to skiers to swimmers. Mother, father and four goslings.

I smile with anticipation. I know what's coming, but it's delicious. I'm like a kid who closes his eyes at a birthday party while his mother places the lit cake in front of him. Sure enough, honking and winging its way directly towards me, the seventh goose becomes visible following the exact same flight path as the first six. As he approaches, the sun turns his jet black plumage into prismatic rainbows.

As he honks, now within earshot of his flock, I can't make out if he's saying "dad, dad, dad" or "do you want a piece of me?" In any case, the goose is clearly a Drake and he overshoots the runway (probably on purpose) and skis in to the flock, causing a ruckus of flapping and honking.

The tears warm my cheeks and stain my shirt. As I go deeper into my heart, I sense the profoundness of my gift of six years with Sam and receive what is probably the most profound message I have ever received:

"Everywhere I go in nature...
and everything I see...
I see Sammy...
and Sammy sees me...."

CHAPTER TWENTY-FIVE

SEARCHING FOR SAM

Thanksgiving Sunday has always been my favorite holiday. The trees are turning, the crisp morning air hints of winter and the mid-afternoon glow of Indian Summer reminds me of July at the lake. Canada Geese fly in formation overhead as friends and family gather for a harvest feast with all the trimmings, including seconds on pumpkin pie.

In Canada, we celebrate Thanksgiving Day, acknowledging God's goodness and mercy, on the second Monday in October. On that date in 1999, I felt deeply saddened by Sam's absence. Often I had taken comfort from walking in the woods, but that morning as I rambled, grief and sadness washed over me like a heavy, dark wave. In the afternoon, we drove to a gathering at the nearby Square Butte Hall. I found it so difficult to go inside and visit that I sought a quiet place to sit and watch the children play on the lawn. Observing their boundless energy, I noticed I felt . . . lighter?

Juli runs up to me and cries excitedly: "Dad, do you see the rainbow?"

I study the horizon in every direction, though I find Juli's question improbable. There has been no rain and few clouds dot the sky. Clearly, she is pulling my leg. "Sorry, honey, I don't."

Sensing my lack of enthusiasm, she comes over,

puts both hands on my cheeks and points my head straight up in the air. To my amazement, I see directly above me, and without a cloud around, a perfect, flawless rainbow with both ends (start and finish) clearly visible. Suddenly alive, I cry: "Wow, Jewel! That is so cool!"

I have never seen anything like it: the rainbow is directly over my head. Laying down in the cool grass, I look straight up at it. The more I stare upwards, the more awed I become. The rainbow looks like a vibrant, multi-colored smile — the kind of smile that a creative six-year-old kid might make if you gave him a box of crayons, a clean piece of paper and said: "Make a smile that will make everyone feel good."

Sam's buddy, Taylor, and his brother were playing nearby. As I stared skyward, a vehicle pulled up. Taylor's uncle Dwayne hopped out, greeted his nephews and produced some bubble gum for the boys — more specifically, two bubble gum tape machines. The coincidence was so bizarre that I thought Jode, Taylor's mother, must have told Dwayne what kind of gum to buy her boys. I asked him: "Why did you pick that kind of bubble gum?"

He shrugged: "Oh, it just seemed like something Taylor would like."

As if on cue, Taylor turned to me and said: "Hey, Tim, look! It's just like what Sam used to give to me!"

Without even trying, the children had lightened my mood.

The rest of the day went better — and, indeed, turned into the best half day I'd spent in a long time. That evening, after Dawn and I had read to the children and tucked them in with hugs and kisses, I sat in the front room reflecting on this memorable Thanksgiving Day. Slowly, as I sat alone, a powerful knowing stole over me. Sam had been a very, very special person to me. He had come into my life to help, assist and guide me, to contribute to my evolution.

In passing, Sam had taught me the hardest lessons I ever expect to learn . . . but also the most profound. To say that he brought me to a new level of awareness, a new sense of connectedness, is to demonstrate the inadequacy of words. Sam taught me that all I need to know is within me. That life is evolution and evolution takes courage and the final lesson was this — somewhere, I had to find the courage to let go, the strength to move forward into the rest of my life.

I rose and went to the door, stepped into the yard and looked up at the starry, starry sky. Standing there, I recalled something my mother used to say to me, something I had forgotten until just now. "Find the brightest star in the universe and when you do... that will be your little sister, Laureen."

As I looked up, I noticed two brilliant stars in close proximity. On this night, it would appear, my creator had positioned my sister and my son side by side. And I wondered: Is Sam's spirit in the rainbows, the butterflies, the sunshine, the laughter, the geese? Is his spirit in the stars? I don't know the answers. But I do know that I will trust and follow my intuition more closely, that I am committed to spending more time being centred and grounded, and that wherever I go, I will keep searching for Sam. I will keep searching for Sam, until I find him...

APPENDIX

A number of articles about Sam's passing appeared in local newspapers. The following are quoted with permission.

Calgary Herald
Thursday, April 8, 1999
Boy pulled alive/from icy pond

By Mario Toneguzzi

A six-year-old boy was fighting for his life late Wednesday night after he spent almost an hour under six metres of icy water in a dugout near Millarville.

The unidentified boy, who lives only a few hundred metres from the dugout, was unconscious, not breathing and had no pulse as he was pulled from the pond, about 70 kilometres southwest of Calgary.

STARS Air Ambulance flew the boy to Alberta Children's Hospital on life support.

"We have to pray for a miracle," said a distraught neighbour minutes after the boy was scooped out of the water from underneath a floating pontoon in the centre of the dugout, which had been used in the past as a fishing pond.

The boy's parents were out of town and late

Wednesday RCMP were trying to find them. Sgt. Wally Purcell of the Turner Valley RCMP said the parents were "just on a nice weekend away."

The boy and his four siblings were under the care of two adults.

Purcell said the male caregiver heard the boy's screams and jumped into the water to try to get him out. The female caregiver called 911.

Fred Stegmeier, associate director for Foothillis Emergency Medical Services, said when emergency personnel arrived they found two winter snowmobile boots floating in the water near the pontoon in the middle of the pond.

He said there have been cases of children surviving "deficit free" after being submerged in water for about an hour.

Stegmeier said a reflex action in the body slows the body's metabolism so it doesn't require as much oxygen. The reflex action is more profound in youngsters than in adults.

Stegmeier said the ice in part of the pond was about seven centimetres thick. The boy was found about six metres under the pontoon.

The boy apparently walked on the ice to the pontoon and fell through the ice near the floating structure.

Stegmeier described the boy as being in "very critical condition."

The man-made pond is just off Highway 549 about 10 kilometres west of Millarville. A blue teepee stands a couple of metres from the highway in the entrance to the acreage.

Neighbour Ernie Geiger said a couple and five children live on the acreage where the accident happened. He said the family moved to the acreage about one and a half years ago. They are living in an older house on the hill overlooking the pond as a sprawling new home is under construction beside it.

"The father spends a lot of time with the kids," said Geiger. "He likes to educate them in the outdoors. They are very responsible parents."

Geiger said he was out "for an evening walk when a lady came and asked if I had seen the boy."

District Chief Gord Agar of the Calgary Fire Department said the boy had been in the water for about 45 minutes when the dive rescue team arrived. They discovered the boy within two minutes, Agar said.

A few minutes beofre 8 p.m., the boy was placed in the STARS Air Ambulance headed for the children's hospital.

Stegmeier said "children should never be around water unsupervised."

The Calgary Sun,
Thursday, April 8, 1999
Frantic search: Rescuers scramble to find boy lost south of Bragg Creek
By Peter Smith and Nova Pierson

A child's lifeless body was pulled from a pond near Millarville last night by Calgary fire department divers, who'd been rushed to the scene by STARS air ambulance.

Early this morning, Foothills Hospital staff were despearately trying to revive six-year-old Samuel Johnson, and were able to get his heart beating again, although it was too early to say whether he would pull through. Rescuers say he'd been under water for more than an hour.

"They're bringing up his body temperature real slow," said Turner Valley RCMP Sgt. Wally Purcell.

Samuel was playing near his home where friends of the family were looking after him while his parents were away, said Purcell.

"He was supposed to come back and never did," said Purcell, who added the parents had been notified of the tragedy last night and were on their way to Calgary from Banff.

One of the two people taking care of him and his four siblings "heard screaming from the raft," which floated in the pond, said Foothills Regional EMS associate director Fred Stegmeier.

That's when 911 was called, sparking a huge ground and air rescue effort by firefighters and paramedics from Calgary, Foothills and Redwood Meadows.

It's believed Samuel had fallen through the ice after walking out to the floating dock on the pond near Hwy. 549 west of Millarville shortly before 6:30 p.m.

After they were alerted, firefighters and paramedics began a desperate race to reach the child, while an ever-expanding rescue effort was launched to back up their effort.

Neighbours drove cars and all-terrain vehicles around the picturesque area, hoping the boy was somewhere else but inside the pond.

But floating in a hole in the three-inch-thick ice were two small winter boots, giving rescuers an obvious point to begin their underwater search.

While firefighters on scene tried using an inflatable boat to reach the hole in the ice where the boy had disappeared, dive specialists in Calgary were alerted.

"Two members of our fire department aquatic dive rescue team were air-lifted by STARS air ambulance helicopter to the scene," said Calgary fire public information officer Garth Rabel.

Within minutes of arriving, the two divers, Dennis Forget and Tom Caves, reached the boy's body 15 feet down in the pond.

Samuel was immediately transferred by

paramedics to the STARS helicopter, which flew him to Foothills.

He was still on the operating table early this morning.

Calgary Herald
Friday, April 9, 1999
Super Sam' dies in hospital/Valiant rescue/of boy from pond/ends in tragedy

By Juliet Williams

A six-year-old who friends called "Super Sam" died early Thursday in hospital. He was pulled the day before from an icy pond southwest of Calgary where he was submerged for nearly an hour.

Samuel Johnson died about 1 a.m. at Foothills Hospital after he was rushed there Wednesday night by STARS air ambulance.

Friends in Millarville, 70 kilometres southwest of Calgary, remembered the boy as enthusiastic and fun-loving.

"He was really spunky, full of energy all the time," said Sam's kindergarten teacher, Trish Draper, who also taught the youngster in preschool.

"I'm so worried about how his buddies are going to take it."

The flag at the Millarville Community School will fly at half-staff in honour of the boy, said principal Tony Hampshire.

A crisis team will be at the shool when students return from spring break on Monday.

Hampshire said the town and school are rallying support for Sam's family. A memorial luncheon, organized by his ECS class, is planned for Saturday at 11 a.m.

"The family weren't long-time residents of the community, but they were very well respected. My phone hasn't stopped all day," said Hampshire. "People are calling to see what they can do or how they can help. Some people just want to bake things (for the luncheon)."

Sam got the nickname "Super Sam" from classmates after he wore a Superman costume for Halloween, Draper said.

"Every time he brought something for sharing, that's what they called him, Super Sam," Draper said.

She said the boy had celebrated his sixth birthday three weeks ago.

"He told his mom that's what he wanted for his birthday — for me to come to the party," recalled Draper.

"When he opened up his gifts, I came over and gave him a big hug. He said thank you for coming to my birthday. That was really special."

Samuel's lifeless body was pulled from a frozen dugout just a few hundred metres from the family home after divers found him in about six metres of water. He was unconscious, not breathing and had no pulse, though medical staff wre able to resuscitate him before he died, Turner Valley RCMP said.

Sgt. Wally Purcell said he was waiting for the medical examiner's report for the cause of death, but he believed the boy drowned.

Tim and Dawn Johnson, Sam's parents, were in Banff at the time of the accident. They rushed to the hospital late Wednesday to be with their son.

The Johnsons, who have four other children, aged 10, 8, 7 and 18 months, have lived on the acreage outside Millarville for less than two years, neighbours said. A luxury home is under construction on the family's quarter section of land overlooking the pond.

Samuel's father, a financial consultant, declined to talk about the incident.

Purcell said the family wanted to thank the dozens of rescue workers who struggled to save their son, who was being cared for by two adult babysitters when the tragedy occurred.

"There may be a possibility that the dog went out onto the ice and he followed him, but we don't know that," Purcell said.

RCMP victim services visited the family. "It's a very sad and tragic thing that's happened. I hope somebody learns from this," said Purcell. He warned that walking on ice at this time of year can be extremely dangerous, as warmer weather causes the ice to be unstable.

Draper said a group of parents and students were on the phone with one another all day Thursday. "We just talk and cry," she said.

"It's going to be hard (on the community)," said Purcell, especially since Sam's siblings have many friends at Millarville Community School. "There are going to be a lot of kids affected."

The Calgary Sun,
Friday, April 9, 1999
Father's warning prophetic/Frantic rescue not enough

By Bill Kaufmann

The grieving father of a six-year-old boy who drowned in a rural pond said he'd repeatedly warned the youngster about walking on thin ice.

On Wednesday night, Samuel Jonnson wandered out onto the ice partially covering the pond on his family's property near Millarville, 55 km southwest of Calgary.

After falling through the ice, it's believed Samuel spent more than an hour in the frigid, murky water before being pulled out by Calgary Fire Department divers and flown to Foothills Hospital by STARS air ambulance.

He died about 1 a.m. yesterday despite frantic efforts to revive him — efforts that at one point appeared to succeed.

"He did have a heartbeat and was breathing... but unfortunately, he didn't make it," said Turner Valley RCMP Sgt. Wally Purcell.

The boy's father, Tim, said his children were well aware of dangers posed by the pond's thin ice.

"We've been warning our kids for a few weeks now to stay off the ice," said Johnson as three of his four other children played around him.

And Johnson hopes the tragedy sounds a warning to others.

"Now that Sam's passed away, perhaps it's a message for other parents and other kids," he said, before kneeling down to softly console two of his other children.

Johnson said it's possible Sam — who attended Millarville Community School — was on a romp with a family dog which might have led to his fatal plunge. "We think he took the dog for a walk and when the dog went out onto the ice, (Sam) thought it was safe," he said.

As one of Samuel's siblings rode past the pond on a mini-bike, a sign on a nearby windmill warns of thin ice.

Friends of the Johnsons were looking after the children at the time of the accident in the pond, which is about 500 metres down the road from the family's log home.

"That (the role of the babysitters) is a difficult thing right now," said Johnson, who was on a business trip when tragedy struck.

Turner Valley RCMP are still investigating the incident, but they said it's unlikely any charges will be laid against the babysitters, one of whom heard the boy's screams from a dock in the cente of the pond and went for help.

"We don't think there'll be any charges — it's just very tragic," said Purcell.

Rescuers spotted two small winter boats floating among the 6 cm-thick ice and were able to pull Samuel out of the water within a minute.

Calgary Herald,
Sunday, April 11, 1999
Millarville Death /
Village turns out / to share family's grief

By Grant Robertson

When a packed gymnasium at Millarville Community School was asked to stand Saturday and pray for one of their own, most of the mourners were already on their feet.

The memorial service for six-year-old Sam Johnson — who died Thursday after falling into an icy pond near his home the day before — had drawn nearly half of the community, 40 kilometres southwest of Calgary.

The 150 people who didn't arrive early enough to claim one of the gym's 300 chairs were forced to squeeze in where they could, lining the gymnasium walls or watching from the doorway.

It was an outpouring of grief. And it touched the boy's father, who coaxed smiles from the gathering during parts of his son's eulogy, but often struggled with tears.

"On behalf of our family and on behalf of Sam, we thank you all for coming today," said Tim Johnson.

Johnson said his son's adventurous side may have been what led Sam to follow the family's dog, Patches, onto the frozen pond.

A few people nodded as Johnson described Sam's

"zest" for sports. Small memorial programs given out at the door included a picture of Sam in his hockey equipment.

After the ceremony, the audience spilled into the library for refreshments.

The Calgary Sun,
Sunday, June 4, 2000
Heroes Among Us/
Calgary Firefighters Awards honour acts of bravery/
Diving in as a team

When lives are on the line, teamwork is the key to success.

Last year, the Calgary Fire Department's Aquatic Rescue Team teamed up with the air ambulance services and police helicopter units to create the Helicopter Operations Team to speed divers to emergencies.

The team was put to the test within days of its inauguration when six-year-old Samuel Johnson fell through the ice of a pond on his family's Millarville-area property the night of April 7.

While crews from the Turner Valley Fire Department and 19 Station in Calgary responded by ground, STARS picked up two CFD divers in downtown Calgary and flew them 60 km to the scene. A little more than 30 minutes after the call, all these crews were on scene and within two minutes of hitting the water, a Heli-Ops diver surfaced with Sam's lifeless body.

STARS flew Sam to hospital in Calgary and despite restoring his breathing at one point, Sam died.

Number 1 Station's Heli-Ops Team "B" Platoon, the Turner Valley Fire Department and Foothills Regional EMS were awarded a Unit Citation for the dramatic rescue effort.

To order your personal copy of **Searching For Sam**,
or to order copies for your friends and family, contact us
directly at:

Website: http://www.searchingforsam.com

E-mail: timrevreal@direct.ca

Super Sam Publishing,
A Division of Cutting Edge Research Inc.,
R.R. 1, Site 1, Box 27,
Millarville, Alberta
T0L 1K0

Tel: (403) 931-2380
Fax: (403 931-4203

For each copy, please enclose $24.57 (includes GST,
shipping and handing).
Credit card orders accepted.
Bulk-order pricing available upon request.

Timothy S. Johnson is available for a limited number
of live presentations or interviews. If you or your group
would enjoy hearing his story in person, please contact
his office using the above information.